UNBROKEN

Martine Wright

UNBROKEN

My story of survival from 7/7 bombings to Paralympics success

Martine Wright

with Sue Mott

**SIMON &
SCHUSTER**

London · New York · Sydney · Toronto · New Delhi

A CBS COMPANY

First published in Great Britain by Simon & Schuster UK Ltd, 2017
A CBS COMPANY

1 3 5 7 9 10 8 6 4 2

Simon & Schuster UK Ltd
1st Floor
222 Gray's Inn Road
London WC1X 8HB

www.simonandschuster.co.uk
www.simonandschuster.com.au
www.simonandschuster.co.in

Simon & Schuster Australia, Sydney
Simon & Schuster India, New Delhi

A CIP catalogue record for this book
is available from the British Library

Hardback ISBN: 978-1-4711-6055-4
eBook ISBN: 978-1-4711-6056-1

Typeset in the UK by M Rules
Printed and bound by CPI Group (UK) Ltd, Croydon, CR0 4YY

Simon & Schuster UK Ltd are committed to sourcing paper
that is made from wood grown in sustainable forests and support the Forest
Stewardship Council, the leading international forest certification organisation.
Our books displaying the FSC logo are printed on FSC certified paper.

To Nick, Oscar, my family and all those who
have been there during my journey.
You know who you are. I would not
be here without you.

Contents

1

The Day

A whiteout. A flash. Out of nowhere. A roar of fierce wind. Metal sweeping and twisting around me, although I don't know that yet. Just as suddenly, it all goes black. Total darkness. What the hell was that? Where am I?

Blackness deeper and denser than mere darkness. A thick, chemical-tasting fog that burns. Something in my head says we've had a crash, but I still don't know where I am. Now a distorted noise comes through. Strangely muffled. Something's wrong with my ears.

And that's when I realise. The noise is screaming.

As the layers of smoke began to clear I could just make out what I was looking at, but it was so crazily wrong I couldn't understand anything. The carriage wasn't there any more. The seat had gone, the floor had gone, the window had gone; just shards of buckled metal rearing up from the floor or hanging in rags and tatters from the ceiling. Something had swung me round by ninety degrees, so that I faced the emergency door between carriages. Except now the door was missing. It was just a hole. I couldn't see anyone or anything behind me because when I tried to move, I couldn't.

Then I looked up and saw something that made no sense at all.

My trainer. One of my new white trainers, which I'd worn for the very first time that morning, was – weirdly – up in the air, four or five feet above my head on top of all this metal. It wasn't white any more. It was red. What's my trainer doing up there? I wondered. I realised later that it was still attached to part of my leg and my foot was still inside it; they were just no longer attached to me.

I thought I'd been looking out of a window onto the tracks but that wasn't the case. I was looking out of a gaping hole made by the explosion. I was literally sitting in a bomb crater. And still people were screaming in pain. It was like a horror movie, and the only thing in colour was the blood.

Nick Wiltshire, Martine's boyfriend, on the overland train from Brighton to London

She's very go-getting, Martine. Very single-minded. It was difficult to have an easy relationship with her. She spent a lot of time going out with work mates and other friends in London, and I'm much more the quiet country type. I was really torn. I'd bought this house in Brighton a while ago. I wanted to spend more time there, as it needed a lot of work. But Martine was happier in London. She's a genuine cockney, born within the sound of Bow bells. The whole family is. I used to joke that they all had pearly outfits at home.

So I was seeing how things went. We'd already split up once but we weren't on rocky ground. We weren't arguing or anything, but I remember getting off the phone with her the night before and thinking, Oh blimey, I'm starting to go up to town again, and we're falling back into the old pattern of me chasing round London after her. I'd gone on at her as usual, nagging a bit. So that was in my head as I took my usual train from Brighton to London that morning for work.

On our way into Blackfriars station, I half-heard the train guard apologise for the delays because of some problem; some kind of power surge. I'd email Martine when I arrived at work to make sure she hadn't been caught up in it.

Martine

I'll always remember the black devastation down there. It was surreal, unbelievable, with all these screams going on ... and then stopping. You don't think, at the time, Why are they stopping? You're just thinking, Get me out of here!

I was leaning against somebody. I later found out his name was Andy. The seats had gone. We were just in this hole. Andy's head was halfway out and he was getting electric shocks from a live wire hanging loose above him. I couldn't see this because I'd been swung round and had my back to him. But I remember feeling him there, and us having this rational conversation.

'We're going to be OK,' he said to me calmly.

'We've had a crash,' I told him.

He knew differently though. He'd been in the RAF, but he didn't tell me what he thought – that it was a bomb. He tried to get up to help the people crying and screaming around us. He attempted to put his legs on the floor but he just fell. That's when he realised there was no floor – just a huge crater. But even if the floor had been there he couldn't have stood up: both his legs was gone. He managed to pull himself back so he didn't fall into the gaping hole.

Hasu Patel, Consultant Plastic and Reconstructive Surgeon at St Bartholomew's and The Royal London Hospitals, about to open her weekly clinic

I passed one of the nursing staff on my way to the clinic at The Royal London in Whitechapel.

'Oh, Ms Patel,' she said, 'something's happened on the underground. There's a closure. There's going to be a lot of delays with the staff coming in.'

'Don't worry,' I said, but then the news began to filter through about an explosion. I realised immediately this would be serious because that word to me meant 'fire', which in turn means burns and injuries. I'm going to be needed in A&E, I thought.

Maureen, Martine's mum, at home in Barnet, looking after her granddaughter

I'd put Matilda in her pram and we were just setting off for Sainsbury's when Paul, my neighbour over the road – he's a cab driver – saw us.

'There's been a big accident in London,' he said. He'd heard through his sister, who worked as a nurse at the Royal Free Hospital. 'She's had to go in, even though she's not due in today.'

'Oh, that's terrible,' I said. You feel sorry for the people involved but you don't expect it to be you.

When we got back from the shop the phone was ringing. It was Grant, my son.

'Mum, what train does Martine get?'

'I don't know, Grant. I don't know what train she gets. Why?'

Tracey, Martine's sister, arriving at work at the BBC in London

I got into work and I knew something had happened. I work for the BBC and loads of people were missing. All the tubes and buses were down. But I didn't even think of Martine first of all. Eventually, I suppose it was about ten o'clock, I called Mum.

'Have you spoken to Martine?'

'No.'

'I've tried her mobile a few times but you can't get through.'

Sarah, Martine's friend and former work colleague, already at her office in Edgware Road, where the bomb that killed six people on the tube was detonated

I knew . . . I knew . . . I can't tell you how many times I've been through all this in my mind, that something was wrong with Martine. And the reason I knew was that Martine didn't call me. I worked at Edgware Road. *Edgware Road*, where one of the bombs went off. If she'd been watching the news she would have tried to call me, just to check I was OK.

Just, 'Hello, you all right? Yeah. Fine. Love you, bye.'

But she didn't. She didn't call. That's how I knew.

Martine

Someone was coming past. A train man. I think to this day about the images he must have been faced with. I was shouting at him through the gaping hole in the side of the carriage: 'Get us out of here! Get us out of here!'

Then a stream of people started to pass us through the tunnel. It was alarming watching them file by, half-obscured by the smoke and the darkness. Like ghosts. Not looking at us. Carrying briefcases, gym bags, rucksacks. Safe, well, walking, normal … going to work like I'd been just a minute ago. I was dumbfounded. If there'd been a crash why were they so OK and we so not? Why were people screaming and injured and dying in our carriage and everyone else just fine? I was completely confused. I couldn't understand. I leaned out of our crater as far as I could, to look further down the train. It didn't make sense. I could see the poles and windows and upholstered seats, entirely undamaged, as though we were in some weird parallel universe. And all the time the other people trudged by until they dwindled to nothing. And we were alone in the dark.

Liz Kenworthy, off-duty policewoman, two carriages away on the same Aldgate train, on her way to a conference at Westminster

I'd just boarded the train at Liverpool Street. We'd hardly entered the tunnel when there was this bang and we came to a violent halt. It wasn't immediately apparent what had happened. Nobody in my carriage was hurt. Nobody was knocked over. A few people began muttering and grumbling in a typically British way, then they started to get a bit annoyed. Nobody was telling us anything.

At first I didn't tell anyone I was a police officer. I hadn't got any of my official kit with me, just a rolled-up copy of the *Telegraph*. That was hardly going to prise the doors open. But after a while I realised something serious must have happened and I had to do something.

'Let me through, I'm a police officer,' I said, moving through the carriages towards the front of the train. There was smoke and dirt drifting towards me and I could hear people shouting. Then I knew something had happened. People were coming towards me, dirty, covered in dust and bleeding. I approached the door they were coming through.

'No, you mustn't go in there,' a chap said.

'I've got to. I'm a police officer.'

Hasu Patel

There was panic everywhere. People were running around. It all seemed very chaotic. I could see that A&E was being prepared to receive a massive influx of patients. Several major resuscitation rooms had been opened up and the first patient was wheeled in. A gentleman. He was being resuscitated. I looked at his legs and they were black. I thought, burn injuries.

'Get the resuscitation schedule ready for burn injuries,' I instructed my team immediately.

Then all I could see was a stream of people coming through very rapidly with really horrendous injuries. Some of them conscious, some unconscious, some sedated. It was just awful. I'm used to seeing trauma in everyday practice but this was completely out of the usual order. People were coming in with mangled limbs. It was terrible.

Nick

As I looked out of the window at work I could see loads of fire engines and ambulances whizzing around everywhere. Martine hadn't answered my email but that was nothing new. She never answered her bloody phone either. I kept trying her mobile. I left a few messages. All I could do was keep refreshing the BBC website, just trying to find out what was going on.

When they started throwing people off buses, I really started to worry. A work colleague had been told by a bus driver, 'They're bombing the buses.' Nothing like trying to keep the public calm.

It was about then I tried Martine's office. They were worried because they hadn't seen or heard from her, so I gave them my number and asked them to give me a call when she turned up. Part of me was thinking she was sleeping through the whole thing, or maybe she was ill. It was weird, but I was still sure she would turn up safe and well.

I spoke to my friends, Richard and Darren. They said, 'She's probably helping people or got stuck in a conversation with someone.' Both highly likely, knowing Martine.

Sarah

I remember everything about that day. It was the worst day of my life. It was no use pretending I could do any work. 'I have to find my friend. I have to do something,' I told my boss, and then joined what looked like a subdued conga of thousands of people, all apparently walking home from Central London. I decided to make my way to my friend Jacqui's house in Cricklewood. She made me a bowl of soup but I couldn't eat.

Desperate to do something positive, we decided to drive round the hospitals. It started to pour with rain. It came down in absolute buckets and, of course, we were totally unprepared. No umbrellas, nothing. We were like drowned rats bursting through hospital doors. Nobody would give us any information until we got to Great Ormond Street and I overheard a man talking to another couple about what was happening.

I jumped in. I was quite rude actually.

"S'cuse me. Are you a policeman? Please, please, can you tell us what's going on? We've lost our friend. We can't find her. Can you help us?'

Maureen

I was watching the news. This number came up for those who knew someone who might be caught up in it all. I started phoning it but every time it just went dead. Too many people were calling. Finally, after literally hours, I got through.

'What's the name of the person you're looking for?' they asked me.

I told them: 'Martine Wright.'

Then it went dead again.

Tracey

Mum talked to Dad and he went out and cut the grass because he couldn't focus on anything. He wanted to be busy. Not think about it. We were probably all doing that: pushing it to the backs of our minds because you couldn't really believe your sister was on one of those trains. By now we knew the chaos had been caused by bombers.

The BBC sent us all home at lunchtime. They asked us to car share, as the whole transport system was down. I took this chap I'd never met before to Watford.

'I hope your sister's all right,' he said, when I dropped him off.

'Yeah,' I laughed. 'She's probably in a pub somewhere.'

Martine

I had no concept of time. I was down there for an hour and fifteen minutes, so the inquest told me, but at the time it felt like forever. Andy had fallen unconscious for a while. I could hear a woman crying, 'My arm! My arm!'

And that's when I remember this figure coming towards me through the gap where the door to the next carriage had been. She had long blonde hair and piercing blue eyes and, in that split second, I mistook her for an angel.

Liz

I peered in and, of course, that's when I found them. The carriage wasn't crushed, as it would have been in a collision; it was torn open. The floor was ripped up, the ceiling was hanging down and there were cables dangling everywhere like spaghetti. The windows were blown out, the door was smashed. There were bits of metal everywhere.

I crawled in and could make out someone, clearly dead, in the bottom of the trench. Another person, a woman, was lying on her back with her arm trapped, screaming. Then I noticed two other people on the right-hand side by the window that had been blown out. There was black dirt everywhere but I could see them by the lights that were on in the tunnel.

The woman looked a bit odd, as though she had been sitting sideways on her seat with her feet on the window-sill. One of her legs had been torn off in the explosion. She was in a really, really bad way but she was conscious. I could see her little face looking at me in the dark. I decided I'd better deal with what I could see and do what I could. I thought, well, help will be here soon.

Nick

I tried Martine's work number again. They were still worried because she hadn't yet turned up. One of her colleagues rang back later to say he'd called her mum, who hadn't heard anything either. So then I left a message with her mum and another one with Sarah. All of us going round in circles. Phones, conversations, empty reassurances.

Something's wrong, I started to think. Something's very, very wrong.

Martine

I kept repeating to the blonde woman, 'My name is Martine Wright. Please tell my mum and dad I'm OK.' Over and over I told her that. I find that quite weird now. I didn't think I was going to die, even as six pints of blood were running out of me. Other people had a different experience. They thought they were going to die in that tunnel. Lying on the track, or in the bomb crater, they had a moment when they said a quiet goodbye to their loved ones, their families. A moment just to themselves. I didn't have that. I was adamant. I kept repeating: 'Please tell my mum and dad I'm OK. I'll see them soon.' I don't know why, but not for one moment did I think I was going to die down there.

The woman had given Andy her jacket to cover him up and I know that she held my hand. There was so much blood everywhere.

'My guts are falling out,' I told her at one point, because I couldn't think how else to account for the ever-deepening pool of blood I was sitting in.

Then she handed me a belt from somewhere and told me to tie it tightly round my left leg. I cannot remember the pain now. I didn't know which leg was worse but she could obviously see. As I was tightening the belt, I thought, I'm like John Wayne. This is like John Wayne in one of those old westerns when he's just been shot in the leg.

Liz

Martine was conscious. She was talking. She was clutching her abdomen saying, 'I think my guts are hanging out.' I could see she was covered in blood but all I could do without a proper first aid kit was keep saying, 'Help's coming. Don't worry, help's coming.' I tied my jacket round Andy's leg but I had nothing left to use on her. It was then another man appeared – young, dark, not British, perhaps Mediterranean.

'Is there anything I can do?' he asked. I thought quickly.

'Yes, there is. Can I trust you?'

'Yes, you can.'

'Then please look after my rucksack, my phone and my warrant card.' I'd lost my pockets, you see, by tying my jacket round Andy's legs, and I couldn't hold onto anything.

'Go and find anything you can, like a T-shirt or a tie; anything to help staunch this bleeding and keep people warm.'

He disappeared as suddenly as he'd arrived. But not long after he was back, with some T-shirts and a belt. I gave a T-shirt to Martine, to hold on her stomach, and the belt to tie round her leg. It wasn't much, but it was something. I wasn't sure that she'd make it but I could try.

Hasu

It was chaos. All the phones had broken down and we were working non-stop in theatre. I told a colleague that we'd need the burns unit at St Andrew's Centre on standby because all the patients would have burn injuries. But then I had a moment to draw breath and do a proper assessment of the first gentleman I'd seen that morning. No, wait a minute, I said to myself, this doesn't look like a burn after all. I got some water, cleaned his legs, and the black came off. This wasn't the effect of burning; he was caked in soot.

We had to stop the resuscitation protocol we'd instituted for burns. That was vital. There could have been repercussions for the lungs. It was a very early lesson for me and I was very happy we'd caught it in time.

Liz

I promised Martine I'd tell her family. I remembered her name but I couldn't write anything down because I didn't have my notebook any more. I was standing in a precarious position on the ripped-up metal floor, bending over Martine and Andy. I knew I was in some sort of crime scene but I just had to concentrate on first aid.

People were walking by, being evacuated. Some wouldn't look at me, although others did, and some passed by as though in a trance. A woman doctor came in briefly behind me and said, 'Don't give them anything to drink.'

'No, I won't,' I said. 'I'm just trying to keep the muck out of their mouths.'

I looked at my watch. It was 9.20 a.m. Where were the rescue services? I couldn't leave. I thought, I'm here now. I'll stay here with the people who need me. But as time wore on I was starting to flag. I'd been down there a long time. I was starting to choke up with all the dirt and I was getting a bit worn out. Then I saw someone and heard a voice.

'I'm a police officer,' it said.

'So am I,' I replied. I'd never been so pleased to see anybody in my life. He, very bravely, had taken the initiative to come down and see what he could do himself before the emergency services arrived. They came – the paramedics and the fire services – sometime later. Martine was still conscious and talking. Andy was getting cold but I didn't have any more clothes to give him. I now felt it was probably safe to leave them.

'This is Andy. This is Martine. And I'm Liz,' I said to the officer. 'Look after them.' But it felt odd, leaving them. I felt responsible for them. But then I thought, No, you'll be in the way and, to be honest, I was exhausted and had ingested a lot of dirt. I had blood all over me.

'Shall I put you out of the window?' a fireman asked, as I prepared to go.

'No, thank you. I'll walk off.'

Martine

I had this sense of everyone leaving our carriage; everyone being rescued except me. It was getting quieter and quieter. I know now that's because people were dying as well as being rescued.

Then Andy went. I knew this because I felt him go and

17

fell backwards into the space where he'd been holding me up. I don't remember Liz – the policewoman my angel turned out to be – being there any more. Everything became indistinct and patchy. I was probably dropping in and out of consciousness.

Someone in the distance was saying, 'Stay with us, Martine, stay with us . . .' Then I remember nothing more.

Nick

By now I was seriously panicked. The lies you tell your-self – *don't worry, she's fine* – just wouldn't stick any more. I'd been calling round all the hospitals in London. Ringing and ringing. If they answered at all they said no one of Martine's description or name was there. Darren came to pick me up in his car and we drove to them one by one. Guy's, nothing. St Thomas', nothing. Bart's, a blank.

Suddenly it all really hit me. I completely broke down at that point. I just realised how much she meant to me. I didn't expect it. I mean, I loved my nan very much, but when she died I just sort of accepted it. I've always been a little bit aloof emotionally. But this was different. I guess I hadn't ever experienced proper grief before and it hit me. I just couldn't take any more. I was sitting in some hospital refectory, I don't even know which one, with Darren and Richard, when I abruptly went wandering off down the corridor. The guys, bless them, came and found me slumped against a wall in tears.

I couldn't work out whether I'd feel better if Martine was at peace or alive and badly injured. The worst thing was not knowing where she was. As we left, it started to piss down with rain.

Liz

There was a body on the track that somebody else was dealing with, so I walked out the same way everybody else had gone. I looked at my watch. I'd been down there an hour. As I came to the surface, there was a policeman standing there.

'I'm a police officer,' I told him, 'and there's two people down there – Andy Brown and Martine Wright.' I was pleased I'd remembered their names. I knew it was important to respect their wishes and pass on their information to somebody official.

But he didn't seem very interested.

'Get on the bus,' he said.

Outside the station there was a double-decker bus waiting to ferry the injured to hospital. Elsewhere there were people being treated in the street, some weeping and wailing. I thought, My goodness, I'm not getting on that bus, so I just walked away. I didn't know where to. I just wanted to get out of the way and call my husband.

There was a little shop. A newsagent. They gave me some water and let me use their bathroom. I looked at myself in the mirror. Oh, my God, I looked awful.

Dishevelled. There was blood on my shoes, on my face, on my jacket. I was covered in dirt. I wiped my face. When I tried to pay for the water as I left, the shopkeeper wouldn't take any money for it.

Hasu

Some people were so badly injured they went straight into theatre. Nobody had names. We didn't know who they were, so we had to give them numbers and code names from the Alpha Bravo alphabet. The most severely injured of all of the victims was number fifteen. We called her 'Hotel Unknown'.

I saw that her legs had been totally mangled. They would need to be amputated straight away; it was plain and obvious. It wasn't a question of saving her legs, it was a question of saving her life. She'd already had one saving grace: we found a makeshift tourniquet round her left leg. In total she lost nearly three-quarters of her blood. Without the tourniquet I'm sure she would have died.

Nick

I decided the only other thing I could do was to go to Martine's flat, as I had a key. Just in case she'd overslept or was ill or had a hangover so bad she'd been in bed all bloody day. I told the blokes to stay in the car because I knew it would be quite messy. Martine wasn't the tidiest woman in the world.

I turned the key and opened the door. It was difficult going in there. I was shouting, 'Hello, hello!' to empty rooms. As predicted, it was a bit of a tip. Stuff from the night before was strewn all over the floor. Typical. One of the first things I saw were the bridesmaid's shoes she'd bought to wear at a friend's wedding in a couple of weeks' time.

The thought that she might be dead was unbearable.

Sarah

After our fruitless rush round London's hospitals in a monsoon, I was in a bit of a state by the time Jacqui and I returned to her house. Darren, Richard and Nick joined us there. At least I was able to pass onto Nick the number of the anti-terror policeman we'd met at Great Ormond Street. He called him straight away. We could hear his end of the conversation.

'Well, she's short, she's got short brown hair . . .'

Jacqui and I looked at each other in despair. 'Nick, for God's sake, tell them something special about what she might be wearing, her rings, a necklace she might have on . . . you're describing half the women in England!'

Sometimes he can be a bloody idiot. I mean, I love him, but I wanted to grab the phone off him and go through everything that Martine might be wearing and what she looked like. Of course I knew she'd be wearing new train-ers. She always did. We used to fight about wearing the latest ones.

Nick

I felt absolutely exhausted and sick. That was partly my own fault. I'd downed two beers and wolfed a kebab to take the edge off my hunger and then felt weirdly guilty about it. Plus they made me feel ill. I was one big emo-tional and physical mess. Every time the phone went off I felt a mixture of hope and horror.

All this time there was a growing voice in my head saying, *There's nothing we can do.* I think I'd resigned myself to it a little bit because, strangely, it was more hor-rible to think of Martine lying somewhere desperately injured than actually dead.

Hasu

In total we treated 208 patients that day. That's how many people came through A&E. I finished very late that night. It was already dark. About ten or eleven, I don't remem-ber. But I was still operating when a young doctor rushed in to ask me about an X-ray he was holding.

'Ms Patel, this lady has a very complicated injury to her leg, but I can't see a fracture.'

'Is there a penetrating wound?

'Yes, very small. About two or three mil.'

I knew what it was – a high-velocity injury from a foreign body. Essentially flying bone. This woman – not Hotel Unknown – had part of someone else's tibia buried in her calf. That happens with blast injuries. Bones and blood products become projectiles and you have to be very careful because suicide bombers have been known to purposefully infect themselves with viruses before detonation. Hotel Unknown, we discovered later, had someone's foot embedded in her leg.

Nick

I tried to sleep that night, but it was pointless. My head was in a whirl. I couldn't fix it to a point and in the end I gave up at dawn and phoned that policeman again. I asked him outright: 'Are there any bodies still on the Aldgate train?' He said yes, to his knowledge, about six or so. My blood ran cold.

I hung up and tried to get myself together. Instead, as I was standing in front of a mirror in the bedroom, I had a weird moment. I thought I saw Martine in the room with me, standing behind me in the reflection. I whirled round and, of course, there was nothing. I dived into the bathroom because the experience upset me so much.

I had a word with Martine in my head then. 'If,' I said sternly, 'there are going to be any spiritual manifestations, then I want them to be to me, but I also want them to be a very, very long time from now.'

Sarah

I was on a mission the next morning. We had to find her and we'd been searching for a photo – a good, close-up photo – to use on the flyers we'd made. God, that had been hard – going through all the pictures from my birthday party the previous weekend, looking at her face smiling out at us.

Jacqui and I were going to tour London, handing out the flyers and trying to get as much attention as we could. Of course, I looked like absolute shit. I was wearing a dreadful green top that I threw on, a disgusting white skirt from New Look, and I hadn't slept. I'd been crying my eyes out. This was not the way I'd imagined my TV debut to be.

But as soon as we arrived in Tavistock Square, our first port of call, we found loads of people doing the same thing. Hair and make-up weren't important any more. Finding Martine was all that mattered.

'Who are you looking for?' asked the TV interviewer.

'Martine Wright,' I said, holding up her picture to the camera, like every other desperate person there. The whole place was swarming with people looking for somebody. It was very, very sad. Traumatic.

Tracey

We got up at 5.30 a.m. the next morning and we didn't know what to do. None of us had slept, but we thought going to The Royal London Hospital again was better than nothing. We all went: me, my mum, my brother, my brother's wife, Alley. We went into reception and this time they told us there were three patients who were still alive and as yet unidentified.

But a huge number of people were there, all of them hoping that one of the survivors would be the someone they'd lost. It was so sad. People were just grasping at straws, I suppose. A policeman came and talked to us, took our picture of Martine, and then moved on to speak to other people.

Nick

The Royal London had set up a room for people searching for their loved ones. But it was like a lottery. Some would never be found alive. Sitting there, it felt like I had a million-to-one chance that Martine would be OK.

Then Prince Charles arrived. It was bizarre. The staff were all lining up outside to be presented to him and I was thinking, I don't give a crap. If Martine's in here somewhere I'm going to bust through that line, whatever His Royal Highness is doing.

A journalist came nagging and I bit her head off. I nearly chucked her down the stairs I was so angry.

Hasu

There was a royal visit on the Friday. Prince Charles came. But I'd been checking the progress of my patients and I realised that the left arm of the woman we called Hotel Unknown had become dangerously swollen and tense.

'We've got to get her back to theatre straightaway,' I said. 'She's got compartment syndrome.' If we didn't operate immediately there was every chance that she would lose her arm as well as her legs.

'But you'll miss the royal visit,' one of my team said. 'Come on, you can postpone the operation for a little. Just an hour.'

No way. An hour would be crucial. It was just overwhelmingly important that I did the operation and I will never regret that decision.

Tracey

My sister-in-law, Alley, couldn't stand it any more. She suddenly said to me: 'Look, why are we sitting here? Come on, Tracey, let's go and look ourselves.'

This was a big hospital. We didn't know where anything was, but, leaving Mum and Grant behind, we

followed the signs to intensive care. If Martine was anywhere she'd be there. Of course there was a door code.
We couldn't get into the ICU without pressing the right
buttons, but we got lucky; a bloke walked out and we
walked in. Not far though. A policeman was on the other
side of the door with a gun.

'What are you doing here?' he said, very unhappy to see
us.

'We're just looking for our sister,' we pleaded.

He told us to get out.

But there was a nurse standing behind him. She looked
at the two of us, two women crying, and said, 'Hang on a
minute. They don't look very threatening.' She asked us
to sit down and spoke to us.

'We've got some people who remain unidentified,' she
said cautiously.

We told her we were just desperate. 'We want to know
if she's here. We *need* to know if she's here.'

'Can you give me a description of your sister?'

We did. Every last detail, including the small mole
above her lip.

She went away and came back.

'Which side of her face is the mole on?' she asked.

My heart did a flip. It was way, way too big a coincidence to think that someone else had a mole on their lip.
Martine . . .

'My God,' was all I could say.

Maureen

'Something's going on here,' I said to Grant, 'because they keep looking over at us.'

A woman, they called her a bereavement officer (which didn't sound good but I didn't say anything), came over and asked us to go to intensive care with them.

'We want your son and daughter to come through, Mrs Wright,' someone said to me. 'We think we may have found Martine. But we have to check. What was she wearing yesterday morning?'

'I don't know. She doesn't live with me.'

'Would she be wearing new trainers, do you know?'

Tracey

The nursing staff were careful to take Grant and I away from Mum before they told us. They were going to let us see the patient they thought might be our sister but wanted to warn us first.

'So sorry to have to tell you, but the patient's injuries were so severe we had to amputate both her legs.'

We went in. Someone was lying there with these contraptions all over her. It was hard to recognise her, not because she was burnt or anything, but she was really, really swollen up. My brother couldn't take it anymore. He was really upset, shouting, 'It's not her, it's not her, it's not her.'

I said it was her. So then they had to call for Mum. I stopped them. I had a terrible thought. 'Look, I can't tell Mum she's got no legs.'

'No, it's all right. We don't expect you to do that. Don't worry, we'll tell her.'

And all the time Grant was banging on the wall, in denial.

Maureen

They told me before I went in. About her legs.

I didn't cry. I just stood there. In shock, I suppose. I couldn't, I really couldn't believe it. But in I went. Grant was there. He was crying and saying, over and over again, 'It's not her.' I went over and looked at her face. The swelling was really bad.

'Look,' said one of the nurses. 'Look, she's got a little mole on her face.'

Yeah, she was right, and there was something else.

'It is her,' I said at last. 'It's her because of her eyebrows.'

Sarah

It was lunchtime, early afternoon, and we were all in Nando's in Old Street – me, Richard, Jacqui, a few others – when my phone went. It was Darren. I stepped outside to hear properly.

'They've found her.' Then he said, 'Listen to me

carefully. She's alive but she's had a lot of injuries. She's lost both her legs and her arm is in quite a bad way. They don't know what she's done to her head and she's in a coma.'

In that split second I was so happy, just knowing she was alive, that my heart leapt for joy.

Liz

I never did find out who that young man was – the one who looked after my rucksack and found the belt for Martine. He didn't come forward afterwards and I never saw him again to say thank you. He was the only person who was brave enough to come into that carriage, apart from the lady doctor. He was like an angel who just appeared one minute and vanished the next.

Hasu

At some point the previous day I'd gone to the coffee room for a drink of water and, while I was there, the news of the bombing came on the television. They were asking: 'Who could have done this?' And I got really, *really* angry. How could anyone have caused this kind of destruction to innocent people who had done nothing to deserve the terrible injuries we were treating? And the deaths. It was just dreadful.

And then I thought, Look at you, Hasu, getting really

angry when you have all these patients to look after. This is no way to cope. You have to redirect all this emotion. I wondered how I should do this and I came up with my own solution.

I stood there quietly and made a vow. I said to myself: *I promise, I swear, that the patients who have come under my care this day are going to walk out of this hospital as they walked onto the train this morning, with all their hopes and dreams.*

Hotel Unknown – although by now I knew she was Martine – would keep her hopes and her dreams.

2

'Hotel Unknown'

My eyes, when I opened them again over a week later, were full of blood. They told me there were no whites at all. Asked me if I wanted to see. I didn't. I was too scared to look. But that was a bit later, when I could vaguely think straight – when I was out of the coma and knew the difference between morphine-induced hallucination and painful reality.

At first I had no idea where I was. For some mad reason I thought I was in a hotel room in New York, and I struggled to understand why a framed photo of my niece and nephew was standing up beside my bed. The thinking was all too much. I closed my eyes again.

Next time I opened them it was dark, except for the glow of tea-lights around my bed – a nice romantic touch from my scrambled brain. A man was there. He was gentle, kind, and somehow I knew his name was James. It was strange. I was in a confused land of drugs and dreams, half-awake, half-unconscious. My hearing was muffled – both my eardrums had perforated, unbeknownst to me at the time – but I could hear this voice speaking quietly and carefully to me.

'Martine, I've got something to tell you,' James was saying. 'You're in hospital. You've had an accident and I'm so sorry to tell you that your legs were so badly damaged we had to take them away.'

I remember hearing the words but not remotely grasping their meaning. No legs? Of course I had legs. I tried to lift my head a little from the pillow, to look down the bed and prove him wrong. I couldn't see clearly and, anyway, it was dark, but my eyes began to adjust to the gloom. I could see one of those waffle-type hospital blankets lying there. Lying flat where my legs should have been. Nothing else was there at all.

Did I cry or scream? Perhaps. I don't remember. I still wasn't properly conscious. I was coming back to life slowly, rejoining the world going on around me after a week in a coma and the multiple operations that had saved my life. In some ways I was through the worst. I'd lost two-thirds of my blood, I was the most badly injured survivor to be hauled from the wreckage of the Aldgate train and yet, by some miracle – and the skill of my extraordinary surgeons – I survived. Down there in the tunnel I was convinced I wouldn't die but now, here, in the intensive care unit at The Royal London Hospital, I felt condemned.

There was a day I was sure I was going to die. I was going into theatre for one more operation – on my arm, I think. But I wouldn't close my eyes. Everyone – my family, the doctors, the nurses – kept saying, 'Go to sleep. You need some rest.' I wouldn't.

'I'm going to die, I'm going to die,' I repeated over and over.

'You're not,' Mum or Dad or the nurses would say. 'You've had loads of operations already. Look at you. You're fine. Don't worry.'

I wasn't having it. As soon as my family had left I asked for a pen and paper from a nurse I insisted on calling 'Ruth', even though her name was Caroline.

'I want to write my last wishes, Ruth,' I said. My last will and testament.

'Martine, you're not going to die,' she said, gently.

'I am going to die, I am,' I insisted. Nothing could shake that belief. Every time I closed my eyes I thought I'd never wake up again.

My family was there every day: Nick, Mum, Dad, my brother Grant, his wife Ali, my sister Tracey, my nieces and nephews, all trooping in, holding my hand and talking about everyday crap, because that's what they had to do to be normal. Just waffling on. I'd caused them so much hurt and devastation already and I felt terribly guilty about that. And now I was going to die.

'Ruth' brought me the pen and paper and I tried to write but I couldn't. I was desperate to tell them that I loved them and I wanted my ashes scattered in Koh Pha Ngan in Thailand, a gorgeous, unforgettable place I'd found on one of my 'gap year' adventures.

Then I had the operation. And they were right. I didn't die.

Drugs, shock and pain coincided, but I mostly experienced disbelief. One morning I'd gone to work, happy, busy, up for a party to celebrate London's success in bidding for the Olympics. The next thing I know I'm lying in a hospital bed, helpless, my legs gone and normal life seemingly gone with them. Every morning I'd wake up having forgotten – then open my eyes and remember. It was like the destruction happening over and over again. It was torture.

God knows how it was for my family having to witness it. For a while they kept the cause of the 'accident', as they called it, secret, but they knew they couldn't keep the real reason quiet forever. On the day they chose to tell me a psychologist was there, and the ward sister too. She was very lovely but stern; you wouldn't mess with her. Mum and Dad were petrified about what they were going to say and how I'd react.

I knew they had something important to announce. They were sitting on either side of the bed, looking intently at me, grabbing my hands. I couldn't guess what it was. How bad it could be? What's worse than waking up in bed at the age of thirty-two and finding you've got no legs?

'We've got something to tell you, Martine,' Mum said. 'It wasn't a train crash . . .' She faltered. But my mum's a strong woman. 'It was a bomb.'

I wasn't really shocked. I'm sure your brain doesn't completely switch off when you're in a coma, otherwise how could I possibly, deep down, have known that already? I'd somehow by then absorbed the news. Maybe I'd even discovered it while the firemen were cutting me out of the train. Mercifully I have no memory of that, and it has never come back. But the guys who were there, a fireman called Ricky, the policeman, the paramedic, have told me since that I was conscious, screaming.

I had survived. That was true. But while I was still in ICU I was seriously nuts from the drugs. I held a very peculiar grudge against one of the nurses.

'Mum,' I hissed once, 'that nurse is stealing my blood.' I could see this poor woman walking around with a denim bag and I convinced myself that was her means of secreting the blood she was siphoning from me like a petrol pump.

Mum was all embarrassed. My so-called whispering was pretty audible.

'No, she isn't, Martine. Don't be silly.'

'She is, she is, she is.' I was adamant. 'It's in her jeans bag.'

I wouldn't let it go. When another nurse came in, I said,

'Where's that other nurse? She's stealing my blood. Have you given her the sack?'

'No, she's gone to lunch.'

God, the poor people who had to humour me. I'd be lying in bed having my catheter changed, never the most delightful of public events, and I'd get it into my head that this was actually happening outside, in the hospital garden. I'd further embellish this nonsense with the belief that a whole crowd of wedding guests was sitting on top of the buildings nearby, eating platefuls of a lovely buffet. Completely nuts.

'Isn't that nice?' I'd say, all thrilled, to Mum and Tracey. 'Look! Alex and Rob are up there. They've brought their guests and leftover wedding food to the hospital.'

There was only one option for my bewildered sister – she had to go along with it. 'Oh yeah, I know,' said Tracey, lying through her teeth. 'We can see them too.'

But in a way it made sense. The wedding of my best friend Alex to Nick's friend Rob was obviously in my mind. The bridesmaid's dress I'd been going to wear was still hanging in my wardrobe, back at my flat, where it had been since our last fitting. My sparkly bridesmaid's shoes were in a box on the floor.

It upset me terribly to miss that wedding, just nine days after 7/7. One of my last nights out was the massive hen do after our final dress fitting. Nick went to the wedding but I have no idea how he managed it. He came to see me in his suit before he went, and showed me the framed photo he was going to give them as a wedding present, a picture he'd taken of the lakes in the Lake District. I said it was lovely and it was. But inside I couldn't help myself thinking, Why wasn't I there? Why has this happened to me? That little voice often buzzed in my brain: *why me, why me, why me? I'm a nice person. Why has this happened to me?* It was only later that I acknowledged my own selfishness. I realised how hard a day it must have been for the people I knew and loved at that wedding because they were thinking about me.

By now, grim reality was starting to break through the trance of disbelief. The doctors had explained they'd had to amputate my legs above the knee. There was no choice. My knees were too torn and badly injured to be saved. That was a fact, but accepting it was so hard. I simply couldn't believe I had no legs. It was almost like being cut in half. I had this feeling that was with me all the time: *my life is over.*

The doctors were wonderful though. Every morning I awoke to the face of Hasu, one of the best plastic surgeons in her field in the world, smiling down at me, telling me how well I was doing. I wanted to live up to her expectations. I vowed I would walk again. I would live a normal life. Then something would come along to knock me down again.

It was good news when I was well enough to be moved from intensive care to a high-dependency unit, the

Harrison Ward. It was small, only six beds, and I arrived there with just one green bag of all my things. My whole life reduced the contents of a plastic bag.

It was a shock at first. In ICU everything is done for you. Here, when Mum and Dad said goodbye that first evening on the ward, I was hit by the realisation of how helpless I'd become. I wanted a drink of water but I couldn't move. I physically couldn't do the simplest thing like reach for a glass of water. I looked at it instead and felt utterly distraught that this was the state of my new life. I'd come back from the dead to be useless.

In quiet moments the question why raced around my head on a loop. Why did I turn my alarm off that morning and give myself another ten minutes sleep? (Although I knew the answer to that one. I'd been out celebrating London winning the 2012 Olympic bid the night before. Wow! Great! I must get tickets to that, I'd told myself as the party mood engulfed us all.)

Why was the Northern line partly down, so that my usual route to work at Tower Hill had to be changed? Why did I take the Circle line, a line I *never* used because it was so unreliable? Why did I run up the escalator at Moorgate and jump in that particular carriage on that particular train? Why was the bomber in my carriage, just a few feet away, with his rucksack?

Did I think that about the bomber? Maybe not. My mind wouldn't go there. I blocked it. But the rest I certainly did. Over and over and over until it felt like inescapable fate. I'd cry buckets. Then pull myself together. The only control I had was to try and stay positive.

At first I thought I must be dreaming when my mum said, 'That was Heather Mills on the phone. She's going away with her husband tomorrow (that husband in those days being Paul McCartney, whom my sister absolutely adored) and she really wants to come in and see you. She's called about ten times. She won't take no for an answer.' God knows how she got Mum's number.

What could I say? 'OK. All right.' And there she was by my bed, two false legs under her arm, very matter-of-fact, telling me all kinds of practical things because, years before, she'd lost a leg in a traffic accident. She told me not to worry – I'd be able to run the 100 metres in less than ten seconds like Usain Bolt when I got out of hospital, which fortunately I recognised as a little white lie, but she was actually great. She gave me a notebook with her personal mobile number in it and said I could write down any questions I had and she'd answer them if I gave her a call. She told me about natural remedy tablets to help restore my gut to normal after all the antibiotics and other drugs. It was the first very surreal experience of my new life.

As she left I said, 'My sister loves your husband.'

She replied, 'Everybody loves my husband.'

How bizarre was that? It gave me a real boost when I needed it. I was trying very hard not to sink into self-pity but I was definitely living in a hospital bubble. I know I was because I was so shocked when, two weeks after 7/7, the family, very cautiously, told me about the attempted second wave of transport bombing in London that mercifully failed to kill anybody. The bombs hadn't exploded properly and the would-be bombers had fled. There was a massive manhunt to find the perpetrators and, in the confusion, the following day an innocent Brazilian man, Jean Charles de Menezes, was shot and killed by mistake. God, what was happening to London?

'Not again. Not again,' I remember saying to Tracey. I was really distressed. I felt terrible. In fact I was feeling really ill. This was the start of one of those nasty hospital bugs – a C. diff infection. It was so bad they had to transfer me out of Harrison Ward and into a room of my own, so the infection didn't spread to anyone else. I remember lying in bed shaking. My blood pressure was so low and my temperature so high they hooked me up to the monitor again. That was a huge psychological setback. And scary. It reminded me of being back in intensive care. I could see Mum and Dad looking worried and trying not to. I felt guilty.

'I will be all right, won't I?' I kept asking. I was on an antibiotic drip, feeling weaker and more depressed than I had when I first woke up from the coma.

'Mum, get the commode,' I'd say every hour or so. That was the cue for everyone to exit the room except Mum. She'd sit in the corner and put the newspaper in front of her face to give me a bit of privacy. It went on all through the night. Sitting there, head in a bucket, at 3 a.m., crying and silently begging for the pain to stop. The 'Why?' questions continued to haunt me.

It was a horrible time. But the very worst was the day a professor – a leader in the field of amputees, I was told – came to see me. I was pinning my hopes on him. I wanted to walk again. I wanted him to tell me I would. Ms Patel had explained that he was coming to have a chat with me and talk me through the possibilities. I was as excited as you can be when you're shaking and sick with a hospital bug. Mum and Dad were there too. We were all ready to hang on his every word.

'I will walk again, won't I?' I asked, seeking immediate reassurance.

He was there for about two minutes. 'You should be able to walk again,' he said crisply. 'We shall have to see. You might not. And you're never going to be able to climb stairs or walk without the aid of a frame or a stick.' And then he was off again.

I was reeling. *You might not.* Those three words were like blows. This was the expert and he was telling me, what? That I might need a wheelchair? That I might need a walking stick for as long as I lived? It was too horrible to contemplate. I looked around the room at Mum, Dad and my brother. They didn't say anything. But I could see it in their eyes: the horrible fear that this was it. I might not walk again – ever.

Ms Patel somehow heard what had happened because she was soon sitting beside my bed, saying, 'Martine, take no notice of him. You're one of the strongest people I've ever met and the first patient to ever come out of a coma smiling.' (I didn't know that. It was probably the drugs.) 'And you have such a strong and wonderful family around you. You'll be all right.'

They all came in then: Beth, the occupational therapist; Claire, the physio. Everyone was saying the same thing. I tried to believe them. But I felt so desperately disappointed and afraid. Drained by the C. diff infection, I didn't have the strength to fight my misery. It was a dark time. I seemed to be permanently clamped to the commode. It was awful. The pain, the smell, the aches in my legs, or what was left of them, still so raw from the double amputation.

I weighed six stone. I couldn't eat. I felt desperate, depressed, and didn't know how I could possibly carry on. Mum could see it in me. I don't know how she knew what I was thinking but she did. She dropped her paper, grabbed hold of my face with her two hands and looked into my eyes.

'Martine,' she said, 'I know how you feel. But think about it. You're still you! You're still here! There were people on that train who didn't survive. There were people who are suffering from brain injuries. But you're still here. You're still you, Martine.'

Never will I forget that moment. It made the difference

between hope and giving up. My mum gave me some of her strength to keep going. It was the restart I needed. I cried and cried but the words sank in and stayed. It was a turning point.

I tried to focus on immediate goals; small signs that I was making progress. A couple of weeks after recovering from the infection I could sit up and reach for my own water. I could balance well enough on the edge of my bed and transfer to a wheelchair. Legs are really useful for balance as well as walking – something you discover when you don't have them anymore.

The next thing on the list would be managing a visit to a hospital toilet on my own for the first time. It would be a significant sign of progress but it scared me. Would I be able to balance? Without legs it would be an incredibly difficult manoeuvre just to get on the seat. They said I was ready – that I'd be able to shift over from wheelchair to seat using my arms. I wasn't sure. But I did it. It was a big step. It gave me hope and then, for the first time, I looked in a mirror and saw myself. The eyes filled with blood. The scars. The unplucked eyebrows. The drastically thin face. The dark rings. The horrified expression. Look at the state of me! I was distraught, crying, hanging onto the sink. I forced myself to stop looking, then washed my hands, dried them on a paper towel and peered around for a bin.

Oh, my God. There it was. In a *disabled* toilet, in a

hospital, specially designed for people in wheelchairs – a pedal bin. Now I'm angry as well as crying, shouting out loud, 'That's ridiculous! How's someone with no legs supposed to use that?' Which then made me laugh. A storm of emotions in one visit to the loo.

My first proper bath was equally upsetting. When Beth, the occupational therapist, mentioned the idea I instantly imagined bubbles, tea-lights and all the comforts that go with a warm relaxing bath. Mum came with me and I was wheeled to an ice-cold hospital bathroom, confronted by this contraption that looked like an electric chair bolted to the side of a bath.

'What the hell is that?' I asked. It was the motorised platform where I'd sit to be lowered into six-inch-deep water. If anything had ever been designed to say, 'You're really disabled, and this is your new normal', it was this. It was depressing and unnatural.

I can see my mum now saying, 'You'll be all right,' with that sing-song cheerfulness that means you won't. I sat there crying, wondering if this was what my life was going to be like every time I had a bath.

It was like this all the time. Up one minute, down the next. At first, much as I absolutely loved my friends, I didn't want them to visit. I felt vulnerable. It was all right for the family to see me, but I just couldn't face the rest of the outside world. Instead, cards and letters from friends and strangers arrived in a deluge. It was amazing and uplifting. I appreciated every one; I can't tell you how much. But there were so many things I needed to do to feel like a human being again.

One of them was eat. My whole family was desperate to get me to eat something. It must have been a huge worry, seeing me so weak and thin. The nurses were suggesting cream cakes to fatten me up. But just the thought made me feel nauseous.

Mum was always saying, 'Anything you fancy? Cake? Buns? Chips? Steak? There must be something, Martine.' I just groaned. Feeling sick all the time from the bug or the drugs was a total appetite wrecker.

Mum would try and get me to eat a bowl of cereal. Dad would be there, reading a paper or listening to *The Archers*. One day, though, I suddenly had a vision.

'D'you know what I fancy to eat?' I said. Zap. Everyone stopped what they were doing. Their eyes were riveted on me. 'I think . . . I might fancy a hot sausage roll.'

Oh, my God, it was pandemonium. Everybody was shouting at once.

'Bert,' Mum yelled at Dad, 'she wants a sausage roll. HOT! Go and get one from the bakery in Whitechapel.'

'I'm going, I'm going. Christ, let me get my jacket on.'

Mum and Tracey literally pushed Dad out of the room.

'Hot! Get six! Hurry up,' they screamed after him. Poor Dad was sent charging down Whitechapel High Street, almost killing himself on the mission to Greggs. We debated the scene.

'Imagine if there's a queue.'

'He'll knock everyone over.'

'He's got angina as well.'

I just lay there and laughed. How can you not love a family like mine? And I knew whether I wanted to or not, I'd have to eat the bloody thing when Dad came back. I managed half of it, everyone watching every mouthful. They'd been waiting days – weeks – for me to fancy something and they weren't going to miss the moment. Good job it wasn't something exotic. Dad was sent out every day after that. I spent a full week on nothing but hot sausage rolls and brown sauce.

Nick and the family, they were there every day, a milling group, sometimes all of them, sometimes just a few, sometimes a mixture with friends thrown in. At first it didn't occur to me how they managed it when they lived right over the other side of London. But then they explained that the hospital had given them a local flat to stay in, something only offered to families in such extreme situations. Mum, Dad, Grant, they'd been there since they found me – at first sharing with people who also had family members in intensive care. Gradually, tragically, those people had no cause to stay any more, which upset Mum and Dad terribly.

I didn't think about it at the time but I must have been incredibly selfish. I was always thinking about me. I didn't imagine what they were going through. Nor Nick, who was practically driving himself mad with work and then three bus trips every evening to be with me, and then three bus trips more to get home ridiculously late. When I think about it now, all these years later, it makes me cry still – their selflessness and their strength. I know I put them through hell. But you'd never know it. They were always telling me stories to make me laugh. Like their first night in this little hospital flat, with its attic, corridors and stairs they couldn't get the hang of.

Mum was all right; she was in a double room and planning to share it with Grant. Dad was supposed to sleep two floors up in the attic. My stepmum, Maureen – who Dad insists on calling 'Maureen Two' – had gone home. Everyone was tired and distracted, so Grant offered to walk Dad to the attic. He led the way out of the door and Dad promptly turned round to get into bed with Mum.

'What are you doing, you silly sod?' Mum said. 'We're divorced, remember! You're the one who's going. Grant's staying.'

'Oh blimey, yeah,' Dad said, but he wasn't sure of the way, so Grant led him off again and then there was a pause – and next thing was they were both back in Mum's room again.

'Now what?' she said.

'Grant got lost,' Dad explained, 'so I had to bring him down again.' So Grant was dropped off and Dad disappeared into the night and I don't think anybody ever knew where he slept, including him.

And there would be good days, like my first trip to the outside world. There was this dodgy old pub behind The

Royal London, so we had a group outing there, Grant pushing me in an NHS wheelchair with a scratchy old red tartan blanket over where my knees used to be. Funnily enough, I've still got that blanket.

It wasn't an easy adventure. It's fine to be sick in hospital, to be limbless, to look weird in your own not-yet-adjusted mind. But when you go out into a situation you've been in thousands of times before and you're different – almost literally half the person you were before in the physical sense – then it's tough.

I treated everyone to a pub lunch and it was fine. It was a laugh. It was a wonderful reminder that life wasn't just confined to a bed in a room in a hospital. But I looked at a group of girls having a drink together in their lunch hour and there was definitely anger in me. This could have been you, I thought. They were completely oblivious, obviously. Sometimes I felt like shouting: 'Do you know what happened to me? You have no idea what we're going through. You have no idea what life can do to you!'

I never did, of course. I feel guilty for thinking like that now but those were the days when the soundtrack, *Why me, why me, why me?* was still playing in my head. Yet I wasn't Hotel Unknown any more. I was still Martine Wright. I knew that.

The unrecognisable woman with two lost legs, a fractured skull, lacerated arms, shrapnel wounds and someone else's foot embedded in her thigh was repairing. I'd still stare at my legs, or what was left of them. They looked pretty nasty and scary, especially the left one, and I struggled to get my head round the fact the rest of them was gone.

There was something else. Something I couldn't bring myself to discuss with Nick for years. I don't really know to this day if it's true but I'll always remember one of the doctors, a kind man I called Major Tom, telling me they had done a routine pregnancy test after I'd been admitted to hospital and it came out positive. I was completely and utterly shocked. I didn't know how to react. I couldn't sleep that night.

The doctor had explained I wasn't pregnant now. They'd done a scan and apparently the lining of my womb wasn't thick enough to suggest I was pregnant still, so I might have had a miscarriage. On top of everything else I could scarcely take it in. I couldn't possibly tell Nick. With all he was going through it could break him.

It was Ms Patel who made it bearable. She said that the positive test might have been a misreading, given all the trauma and drugs I'd been subjected to. Perhaps she said it out of kindness to help me get over it. I'll never really know the truth.

Reality had a habit of shocking me. It's understandable that people were always trying to protect me; keeping things quiet that they thought would upset me. But sometimes I'd discover them by accident. I will never forget the jolt of horror I felt when I picked up a random copy of the *Sun* on one of my precarious trips to the hospital gym for rehab. On the front page was a gallery of fifty-two passport-sized faces and above it a headline: 'The Victims of 7/7'.

My God. I didn't know. I was stunned. How could I not have known this? The number was incredible. They looked like me: ordinary people just going about their day. Students, workers, mums, dads, daughters, sons. All those people can't be dead! That could so easily have been me. And the ages of the men and women who died. So young. So many of them younger than me. I felt a weird combination of guilt, sadness and, I have to admit it, relief. It was also the beginning of a feeling I have never lost: that I had to try to make the most out of the life remaining to me. I'd been in mourning for my old self. Now I had a different perspective. It dawned on me then, as it still does, that I was one of the lucky ones.

There is a photo of us all somewhere, the survivors who were treated at The Royal London. I can't recall why it was taken now. Maybe one of us was going home and wanted a souvenir of our hugely emotional time together. I've still got it somewhere. God, I look weeny. There's a grey tinge to all of us, but we're smiling.

Still Ms Patel visited me every morning. The dedication she'd shown by missing Prince Charles's visit to save my arm never lessened. I know that without her being so on the ball I could have lost that arm as well. It was a while before the bandages came off and I saw my arm for the first time. It was bright, bright pink and very scarred. I looked like the victim of a shark attack. On the plus side, it was still there. It was just one of the many reasons that I shall always be so grateful to that wonderful woman.

She was always trying to minimise the physical trauma despite the number of operations I needed. One morning she arrived to tell me: 'We have to do another small operation on your arm. If it was anyone else I would have to take them to the operating theatre to do it, but I think you're strong enough for me to do it here, in your room, under gas and air.'

'OK, right, fine,' I said. I trusted her completely.

Grant was there in protective big brother mode. He volunteered to help. The gas and air had a slightly weird effect on me. I saw smoke writhing along the ceiling. I think it must have been some kind of post-traumatic stress reminding me of the tube train again. The sound of a helicopter did the same thing to me, which wasn't ideal considering The Royal London had its own helipad.

'Can you see that smoke up there?' I asked him, but he didn't seem to be paying any attention to me. He was gazing with a stricken look at the gaping hole where Ms Patel was operating. I watched as the blood drained from his face. I thought he was going to keel over. Then he grabbed the gas mask out of my hand and stuck it over his nose.

'I'll have a bit of that,' he mumbled, swaying.

It was a moment typical of the tragi-comedy that hospital seemed to be. Laughing one minute, agonising the next. Some nights on my own I'd lift the blankets and gaze at what remained of my legs. The doctors had tried so hard to save them but my left leg was completely destroyed and they knew they had to amputate above the knee. They thought they might be able to save the right knee but in the end they couldn't. I had to accept it. But the grief was still there and I wasn't alone in that.

Dad was with me one day in my room, watching television. Mum had gone out somewhere, so we were alone. I started to get a little upset.

'I just want someone to tell me I'll walk again,' I said. I was crying. I could see Dad's lips trembling, so I quickly tried to be cheerful. 'But at least I'm still here.'

By now there were tears spilling down his cheeks. He held my hand.

'Martine,' he said, taking my hand. 'You do know that if you'd died, I'd have died too.'

I only have to think of it, even now, and it makes me cry.

Nick always teased me about my family. Him and his pearly suit jokes. He's right though. The cockney spirit is alive and strong in the Wrights. He's very different, a gentle soul, far more at home in the country than a city, and when you think that we were only boyfriend and girlfriend – nothing more than that – his loyalty and kindness were little short of miraculous.

I hadn't long been out of my coma when I introduced him to one of the nurses as my fiancé. I claim it was the drugs. Actually, it *was* the drugs. I was completely away with the fairies at the time and, for some reason, I had blessed him with our engagement. He must have been aghast while I smiled at him obliviously.

Later, Mum told me he had come charging out of the ward and grabbed her.

'Christ, help, Maureen. Martine thinks we're engaged. What should I do? Do I need to go out and buy a ring?'

He'd been in so many panics. First, not knowing where I was, then discovering how injured I'd been, and now I'd presented him with a different type of trauma altogether – the discovery that he was engaged to be married. Of course it was funny but what a bloke! I can think of others who would have jumped on the 205 bus and never been seen again.

Slowly but surely I was progressing. The stitches were removed from my legs, an experience so painful that I had to clutch Mum's hand and, for some bizarre reason, sing 'What's the story in Balamory?' over and over again. Just why the theme tune to a Scottish pre-school kids' TV programme helped me endure the excruciation I have no idea.

After eight weeks I was well enough to be considered for transfer to a rehab hospital in Roehampton. That made me nervous. It seemed to me like a huge step into the unknown. Before I could fret too much about it I was told I had a visitor who had a special reason for wanting to visit me. This was Ricky, one of the firemen who came to my rescue and one of the first of the emergency crew to reach the people in my carriage. Of course I wanted to see him. I wanted to thank him. I wanted to know what had happened; as much of it as I could stand.

He was a good-looking young man, visibly moved by the whole thing. He had just visited Andy, one of my fellow Aldgate survivors, the one I found myself leaning against and talking to after the explosion. He told me that Andy was doing well, really positive, which was great news. Then he told me the details he recalled.

Before they reached the scene, he and his team had assumed that the problem lay with a couple of small explosions from the discs under the train (as this has happened before) but when they saw hundreds of people being evacuated from Aldgate Station, they knew it was something more sinister. When they reached our carriage – or what was left of it – they were shocked. They had no real equipment, as they didn't know it was a bomb. That came later. But he stayed there working to free Andy from the wreckage while another team worked with me.

It was difficult and painstaking. What remained of my left leg had been fused to the side of the carriage by the heat of the explosion. They worked on, aware of the warning that there might be a secondary device, but they refused to evacuate themselves without us. They didn't know what type of bomb it had been or whether they were breathing in toxic fumes. They carried on. I couldn't help but cry again hearing all this. He didn't want to upset me but I told him to carry on.

He told me that a yard away from Andy and I three people died, including a young female graduate of twenty-three. He had to carry her out. They had a pretty good idea where the bomb detonated. There was huge hole in the floor and ceiling near the door. He didn't say so, but I gleaned that the body of the bomber had been found there too.

He reckoned the glass panel next to Andy saved us both and confirmed what I'd always thought – that I was the last one in the carriage to be carried out. He said I was screaming my head off with the pain. I remember nothing of that, thank God. I must have just switched my brain off. It was gruelling hearing all this but I needed to. Perhaps when you know something in detail, you can start to deal with it.

I didn't have long to dwell on it. Four days later, despite one last dose of MRSA, I was on my way to the rehab unit in Roehampton to find out if I could walk again. There were more tears, but not for myself this time. It was so emotional to be leaving all these extraordinary, kind and wonderful people – the doctors, nurses, physios, psychologist, therapists, all of them – who had helped me, literally, come back to life.

It was the last day of August when I said goodbye to my fellow patients: Thelma, Andy, Philip, a huge guy who'd survived the Piccadilly line explosion, and Kiera, who lost her arm in my carriage on the Aldgate train. I vowed I'd see them again. They were friends. Philip kept saying, 'I'll miss you,' but I told him we'd know each other forever. It was the positive thing to come out of all this.

I got in an ambulance and was crying again. I felt so scared. I had no idea what would happen next.

3

Finding My Feet

I entered a new world of limbless people. Everywhere you looked there were unattached legs. Prosthetic ones. Wooden ones. Propped up against walls, on racks in the gym, or just lying around. This was the rehab hospital where I was to spend the next ten months of my life and I can't say I was entirely comfortable about it. I'd arrived at Queen Mary's, Roehampton by ambulance in my rickety old NHS wheelchair, as unsexy a contraption as was ever invented. Mum and Tracey were with me, but I was nervous. Was I ready for this – new people I didn't know, the trial of trying to walk again? I wasn't even sure I could sit on a toilet yet without falling off.

Then someone shouted, 'Come on, Martine, time for dinner.' So, telling Mum to stay where she was in case I needed her, I wheeled myself down a corridor to the room that would become the centre of my universe for almost a year. Picture this: a glorified Portakabin from the 1960s, green flock wallpaper, untouched since the Beatles were singing 'She Loves You', a large dining table for the patients, a hatch through to the kitchen where shepherd's pie and peas was about to be served, and pictures everywhere of Sir Douglas Bader.

The unit was named after him, aptly: the flying ace who lost his legs in an aerobatic display accident yet became a celebrated fighter pilot in the Second World War. Both his legs were amputated – one below the knee, one above – after his accident in 1931, and I particularly liked the note he made of the event in his logbook: 'Crashed slow-rolling near the ground. Bad show.'

An array of different people – different ages, different injuries, different numbers of limbs – began to congregate. Among them: Terry, an older man, who'd lost one leg from diabetes; Doris, who was lovely and reminded me of my nan, who I think lost a leg due to an ulcer; Joyce, an amputee for the last twenty-five years who still wore legs despite being in her seventies; Graham, who'd had an accident at Wimbledon station when he fell on the track and a train went over his leg; Jenny, a young girl who'd had a motorcycle accident and Kelvin, an ex-Marine who injured his leg in a training accident. He was a real mickey-taker.

Then there was Peter, who I guessed was a professor of some kind, and his wife, who wasn't a patient at all but joined in because she was recovering from brain surgery. I didn't know that at the time.

We sat down to eat and I was instantly involved in one of the most random, meandering, downright mad conversations of my life. People would start off with a thought, then they'd veer off on tangents and some of them weren't really listening to each other at all. I thought, Whoa! What have I come into here? But it was polite and harmless. Everybody must have known why I was there but studiously avoided any mention of it. Just: 'Where do you live?', 'How are you?', 'Was that your niece and nephew?' The sort of stuff the English use to avoid saying anything personal.

Then Peter's wife, mid-forkful of peas, just came out with, 'So, Martine, how was it to be blown up?'

I was shocked. I didn't know how to react. I laughed nervously, thinking, How dare you ask me that? I probably answered that it had been quite unexpected, while Peter had a go at her in a loud stage whisper and all the others started talking at once.

After pudding with custard I went back to my room and said to Mum, 'You've got to get me out of here. This is some kind of nut house.' But within two weeks those crazy conversations would be the most normal thing in the world and that funny little prefab universe felt like home. It was like a ready-made family of mums, dads, aunts, uncles, older brothers and sisters. It was mad but it was ours. I secretly named us 'the Dysfunctional Waltons'.

It was an alien world but not a frightening one. If anything it was like a comedy drama – *Carry On Doctor* with loose arms and legs thrown in. I kept expecting to see Sid James come round the corner in a white coat and stethoscope with Hattie Jacques in a matron's uniform beside him. But we had plenty of comic stand-ins to entertain ourselves. And I'd made a friend.

I'd first noticed Jeannette in the gym at The Royal London. I was in there doing my physio exercises one day when a phone rang. That old Nokia tune blared out and I turned round to see whose phone it was. There was this black woman – like me, with no legs – with a left arm that stopped at the elbow, and no fingers, just three short stubs, on her right hand. It was the first time I'd seen someone with injuries worse than mine. From a self-centred perspective it gave me hope that people could survive with even greater difficulties than the ones I was confronting.

I probably smiled or said hello, but she was very quiet. Not intimidated; just aware that everyone else there had been involved in 7/7 and were understandably pally with one another. But I knew she was going to the same rehab as me, so I took the chance to say, 'See you there,' when she went on her way.

By coincidence we had rooms side by side and it wasn't long before Maggie, our physiotherapist at the unit, decided to call us 'the twins'. Never mind that one of us was black and the other white. It made sense to us. It was living on that ward which broke the ice – the whole unreal situation; the sheer randomness of it. And we did everything together. We were at the same stage of rehab. We were almost exactly the same age. We both had cool friends and the same sense of humour.

She'd get up, try to walk, fall over. I'd laugh.

I'd get up, try to walk, fall over. She'd laugh.

We'd go round Asda together, once we'd progressed enough to be allowed out for a trial shopping trip. She'd push me in one of those trolleys adapted for wheelchairs and then we'd reverse it and I'd push her, to the bemusement of our fellow shoppers. You had to see it to believe it; both of us barely four feet tall. One big tangle of wheelchair, trolley, crutches, walking sticks and prosthetic legs. There was scarcely any room left to put the bloody shopping.

In the gym we'd do dance routines, have sing-songs, do our pelvic floor exercises together. To find another woman, another above-the-knee amputee, what were the chances of that? Few injuries like that happen to women. Among men, they're more common, what with wars and motorbikes. So we were unlucky people, Jeannette and I, but lucky to have each other.

Jeannette wasn't injured in 7/7. Her misfortune was entirely different but just as terrible. A very clever woman, she had been working on developing a meningococcal B vaccine and accidentally became infected with meningococcal bacteria.

It was great having a real mate to share with but I was still struggling with my own reality. I'd wake up in the morning, look down, and expect my legs to be there. I'd think for a split second: *What's going on?* Every morning I was struck with the realisation that I no longer had legs. It was like daily amnesia. It happened to other people too. They'd wake up, jump out of bed and fall on the floor, forgetting they'd no legs to stand on.

Over and over again, I'd wonder, *Why was I on that tube? I'm a nice person, a kind person, so why did that happen to me?* Then I'd shake myself up: *But it did, so I need to deal with it.*

The first time I went down to the gym, just to see the place before the hard graft of learning to walk again began, an NHS photographer was there to take pictures of my wounds – for records and training purposes, they said. Fame at last. So, if not my face, then my legs were destined to have a starring role across the country. How glam.

The gym isn't there any more, it was replaced by a spanking new hospital. But I can still picture it. The yellow lighting. The breeze-block walls. Rows of rails to hold onto, as we took our first tottery steps on, well, how do I describe those 'rockers' designed to begin the process?

They're not cutting-edge technology, put it that way. The first time I saw them I burst out crying. Maggie held them up for my inspection and they looked like something my dad might knock up in his garage with a bucket, duct tape and an old metal belt. They were so ugly and utterly alien. The idea was that I'd lower what remained of my legs into the twin buckets, buckle myself in tight with a big metallic belt and 'walk' on the bit at the bottom that looks like a club foot but is curved backwards so you can 'walk' on them in a rocking motion.

They're short to raise your stability by lowering your centre of gravity. I was pretty short too now, having lost most of my legs. I was looking at the world from a very different, and significantly lower viewpoint. I've got a hilarious picture somewhere of my dear friend Sarah Jones coming to visit me. My *tall* friend Sarah Jones, who's wearing high-heeled cowboy boots while I'm somewhere down round her ankles in my rockers gazing up at this giant. It was sadly comical.

'These are what you're going to walk on,' Maggie said firmly, once I'd finished crying.

It was 8 September 2005 when I took my first steps. I know that because I kept a diary. I called it 'D-Day'. I was called at 1 p.m. to the Prosthetic Centre, another dated area of the unit, where Maggie met me with a prosthetic leg specialist to try out my first pair of rockers. They pushed me into a room where I was confronted by 20-foot-long handrails.

My first pair of rockers was brought in and they asked me to fit myself into them. They were far from the most comfortable things in the world and pinched in sensitive places. But after a bit of swearing I took the first two steps of my new life. Despite the overwhelming 'ouch' factor it felt great.

I stood up and felt really dizzy because I hadn't been upright for two months. 'I think I'm going to faint,' I said to Maggie. She told me not to worry; that was normal. I clung on like grim death to the rails. My arms were taking a lot of the weight. These metal things were the most alien contraptions you could imagine. Awful, sweaty, nasty things.

I'd 'walked' no distance, just a few feet, but I felt absolutely knackered. They say walking on two about-the-knee prosthetics takes 280 per cent more energy, never mind rockers, but I reckon it's more because you have to concentrate so fantastically hard all the time, and even more so on uneven or slippery surfaces.

I wondered when I would feel these legs were part of me. I couldn't control them, and when I caught sight of myself in them it was like looking into a hall of mirrors at a funfair. Me, but a distorted version of me. That was my new reality: a woman who'd walked into a hall of mirrors and would never get out again. I think that's why I felt so depressed at times still, and why I dreamed, sometimes night after night, of having my legs whole again. Asleep I was whole. Waking up and remembering, day after day, was so hard. Even now I still have legs in my dreams.

Another problem was the pain. I was slowly being weaned off the morphine but there were, apparently, bone spurs growing where my legs had been amputated that might need another operation. They already knew that I had bones from someone else's foot embedded in my thigh from the force of the explosion. They also knew they weren't the bomber's, thanks to DNA tests, which was a massive relief. These bone spurs were different, though, and the cause would have to be investigated.

But what was one more X-ray compared to the progress I was making in my walking? I'd graduated after a while from the bars to walking round the gym holding one stick and one tripod (a stick with three legs for better balance). Maggie would watch me like a hawk and Mary, the physio assistant, would help by saying: 'Stick, leg, stick, leg,' to remind me which bit to do first. We'd get in a muddle sometimes. She'd suddenly start going three times as fast to keep up with me, and then I'd try to go faster to keep up with her. Then I'd nearly fall over laughing. Actually, I *would* fall over laughing.

In terms of our accommodation, only Jeannette and I had rooms with our own bathrooms attached. My room was gradually being taken over by cards and get-well notes. It reached the point where you couldn't see the wallpaper at all. That room was my whole world. But after about six weeks, Debbie, the hospital administrator, came to see me and told me that I might have to move out.

'We've got a private patient coming,' she explained, 'and they need a room with their own bathroom. We're going to have to move you.'

I was distraught and, by this point, probably institution-alised. You get so used to being in one place – it's your nest, your comfort, your safe haven, and the thought of being turfed out of it worried me far more than it should have done.

'When's this guy coming?' I kept asking anxiously.

I knew it was a guy, about fifty-five-years old, and would soon discover he must be one of the most kind-hearted people you could ever wish to meet. Chris had suffered a motorcycle accident, not by being a twat, but by being a Good Samaritan. As he was riding along, he'd seen a woman with a bike looking lost by the side of a dual carriageway. He stopped to help her, climbed off his bike and a car bashed into him. He lost his leg by doing a good deed.

He arrived and was shown my room. I wasn't there but someone told me about it later.

'Whose room is this?' he asked, looking at the hundreds of cards.

'It's Martine's,' they said.

'Why has she got so many cards?'

'Well, she lost her legs in the 7/7 tube bombing.'

He welled up and said, 'I can't take this room from her,' and he was true to his word. He had one of the single rooms with a shared bathroom and left me, hugely grate-ful, to my room.

God knows what he thought of the company but as a group in that crazy place we did all get on really well.

Jeannette and I were still being competitive, to see who could make the most progress. To bring us on further we were assigned a mentor and, in my case, that was Steve, our Superman – a high-flying financial director, a dad with a couple of kids, who had done Ironman and a few triathlons when he caught cryptococcal meningitis. He had both legs amputated above the knee, like me. But that was a year before. Now he didn't use a wheelchair at all and was on 'sea-legs'. He was going to be my mentor.

I'm not kidding. I really did think I was progressing to something called 'sea-legs'. I assumed it was descriptive of the wobbly way I'd feel, as I learned to walk on them. Idiot. In fact they were 'C-legs', as in 'computerised'. They had microchips in the knees that could bend and, if you sent them the right instruction, they made walking a much more natural process than the old rockers.

In theory.

I've still got the footage of serious tutorial sessions that descended into farce and hilarity as the knee of one of my C-legs decided to lock solid and straight while I was trying to learn how to get up from the floor.

'Do you want to stop?' Maggie asked, sensibly, as I was rolling around like a beetle on its back.

'No! Hang on a minute,' I puffed, stubbornly, all twisted up, half on the floor, half off it, with this prosthetic leg stuck out at a right angle while Steve vainly tried to make it behave. This went on for some time, believe me. But the mishaps along the way were all part of the learning process, and so I slowly learned to stand on my own two (fake) legs again.

The C-legs were pretty amazing. They used sophisticated sensors to determine where they were in space at all times. They made precise adjustments at every moment of every step. In an ideal world they would let me easily navigate ramps, stairs and nearly every type of challenging surface – even when walking backwards. That's what it said on the tin. But after the low rockers you're suddenly about two feet taller and wobbly. I'd need to practise, practise, practise to be confident.

That meant I'd fall over, fall over and fall over. What the hell, I had to keep going and, if they hurt, which they did sometimes – at the point where bone spurs were growing on the end of my stumps – then I'd somehow have to bear it. There were times, I admit, when I chose the wheelchair as the easier option, but I'd learned by now that perseverance mattered. I'd promised myself in hospital I'd learn to walk again. No matter how hard or how painful, I would.

I'd reached such a point of independence by the end of September that I was allowed to go home and spend the weekend with Nick. This was a huge and challenging event for me. I realise now it must have been the same for him too.

Nick had been coming backwards and forwards to visit me in a clapped-out blue Vauxhall Astra he'd bought off a friend of my mate, Jenny. Roehampton couldn't have been more inconvenient. He was still working at Somerset House, in a job he hated. He was living in my flat in Crouch End, filled with my stuff – including loads of shoes and especially sneakers. How could he not have found that a bit weird? And then he was driving at night in the rush hour to and from one of the most gummed-up areas of London to visit me.

The miracle is that we went out together at all. A greater miracle is that he stayed and supported me through the whole terrible ordeal. He could have walked away. Many men would. After all, I was just his girlfriend when 7/7 happened.

So Nick was going to take me home for a couple of days – my first escape from hospital in months. Not to my flat in Crouch End, because I would never have managed the stairs, but to Dad and Maureen's bungalow, as they were going away.

It was so lovely. We just chilled out and cuddled up, although it was a bit weird seeing everything from a different perspective. I was lower; everything else was higher – ceilings, cupboards, Nick.

It didn't matter. I treasured those weekends. Tracey always picked me up for the long, two- or three-hour stop-start drive round the M25 in the rush hour that would probably take about fifty minutes on a good run. I didn't care. It felt exhilarating to be out in the real world again. Then Nick would drive me back on Sunday evenings, when I'd be in a very different mood. Subdued to say the least. Like that back-to-school feeling when you're young – only a thousand times worse.

It was during one of these weekends that the first story of my recovery appeared in the national newspapers. A *Guardian* journalist had come to see me at Roehampton and, on the very first Saturday morning I was home with Nick, I was confronted by a picture of myself on the front page of a newspaper. In a wheelchair, looking thin and sad. It upset Mum when she saw it. The *News of the World* had written a big piece on me too, so I was splashed all over their front page on the Sunday.

The whole media thing was a bit mad. I was even 'papped' a couple of weeks later. Word must have got out that I was home for the first time because the *Sun's* front page had a picture of me getting out of the car in Dad's street. I didn't know anything about it. They must have looked him up in the phonebook – Albert Wright, Edgware – and waited, hiding up the street on the off chance I'd go there.

Then *Grazia* did a piece on me but, even though I didn't want it, they used a picture of me with legs, from a time before the accident. That really upset me. I wanted to sue them. I wasn't nearly ready to be confronted by memories of how my life once was; how my body once looked. It was one thing knowing privately what had happened but quite another seeing it splashed over the newspapers. I'm not shy, as is probably evident. But it all takes some getting used to. And I wasn't ready yet.

Clearly though, the time was coming when I would have to face real life again. A big event was coming. It was a huge thing for me. It would mean crowds and venturing into London again, only four months since I'd been pulled alive, just, from the tunnel in Aldgate station. It was very daunting but I had to be there.

The Service of Remembrance at St Paul's Cathedral was going to be held on 1 November 2005 for those who died, those who were injured and those who came to our rescue on that day in July. It was the first time I'd properly ventured into the outside world, still in my dodgy yellow NHS wheelchair, with the old scratchy red blanket over my legs.

The day had begun with a phone call from Sir Trevor MacDonald – he was making a programme about me at the time – just to say, 'Martine, how are you?' That was typically thoughtful of him. But I never could quite get my head around having 'Sir Trev' as a number in my phone. He's alphabetically next to 'Sis' in my contacts list, and I'm pretty sure I've accidentally called him a little tipsy from time to time trying to reach my sister.

My family came with me to the service – Nick, Mum, Dad, Tracey, Grant – and the police drove us there in a minibus. I remember the excitement of driving really fast down the bus lanes and then the shock of seeing what looked like thousands of people gathering around St Paul's. Once we were in, we sat near the front, where I could see the Queen and the Duke of Edinburgh. The music was beautiful. The words were moving. But my most vivid memory remains the sight of the families who had lost their loved ones. My life had been irrevocably altered but what had happened to them was far, far worse. One random choice on an everyday morning and everything is different forever.

I met Andy that day, a policeman who had been with me in the train carriage, introduced to us by our wonderful liaison officer, Jim. I couldn't remember Andy, which upset me greatly.

Then he said, 'Do you remember someone saying, "Martine, squeeze my hand"?'

'Yes,' I said. I did remember. It suddenly clicked. So that was him.

Jim later came to visit me in Roehampton and told me that Andy had shown him his hand after I'd left them at the service. 'This is what Martine did to me,' he explained, and a set of scars was still clearly visible. Oh God, he'd given me his hand to hold in that carnage on the train and I'd dug my nails into him so deeply that the marks were still there. The memories of that agony have never come back, for which I am profoundly grateful. And very sorry for Andy too.

A woman came up to me after the service.

'You don't know me,' she said, and told me her name.

'Lovely to meet you,' I said. 'Were you involved that day?'

'My husband was. We lost him and I have two small daughters. One's three and one's five.'

We chatted. Hers was the story that really galvanised my campaigning on behalf of all those affected by 7/7. She was going to receive £8,000 in compensation for losing her husband – the father of her two young children and the breadwinner of the family. She couldn't go out to work because her girls were so young – and traumatised. If she didn't work, how would they financially survive?

It was a classic Catch-22, imposed on a grieving family. I was outraged. Her story affected me and would become one of the chief reasons I took on the government about the levels of compensation paid to all those who suffered because of 7/7. That would come later. For now, it just made me sad and angry.

My friends and family could tell when I was overwhelmed with unhappy thoughts. They did everything they could to cheer me up or just keep me company. There were times when they were just so ridiculous I couldn't do anything but laugh.

Michelle springs to mind. A dear, longtime friend, and godmother, she is obsessed with celebrities. There isn't a *Heat* or *OK!* or *Hello!* magazine she hasn't read from cover to cover. You can ask her anything. She knows the lives of soap actors and film stars better than they know themselves. She's great company and would join a gang of my other friends from time to time to take me out to the local pub, The Red Lion.

On this particular day, I'd finished up in the gym, had

my shower and was awaiting their arrival with impatience. No sign of them. Not happy with the delay I rang Michelle on her mobile.

'So, where are you?' I asked her, a bit irritated.

'Oh, don't worry, we're here now. Just coming up to the man on security.'

'What do you mean, "man on security"? This isn't a bloody prison. There isn't one.'

'Yeah, it's fine,' she replied, not really listening. I could hear babble in the background.

'Oh, Martine, they don't know your name.'

'Ask them which hospital you're at. Is it Queen Mary's?'

'Hold on. Wait a minute . . . Oh!' I could hear more hubbub and then a squeal. 'Oh, my God, it's The Priory!'

Never mind seeing me. Nothing could have delighted her more. It was with great difficulty that all my other mates persuaded her not to dash in and trawl the place for rehabbing superstars.

I knew what had happened. 'You're in the wrong road,' I said wearily.

Fortunately, the 'man on security' did his job, told her to scarper and, finally, I got my trip to the pub.

A lot of the laughs were bizarrely accidental. Mum and Dad came with me for an X-ray one afternoon. I thought it was for an X-ray on my legs but the radiographer said something about a bowel obstruction. I was just about to protest and say there must be a mistake – I didn't have anything wrong with my bowels – when Mum, not even looking up from her newspaper, said casually: 'Oh yeah, they thought you had a bowel obstruction but it turned out to be a thermometer up your bum.' She carried on reading as if she'd just said, 'I'll have two sugars with that.'

'What?' I tried to grasp the important facts here. 'You mean someone took my temperature and left the thermometer up my arse?'

'Yeah, that's right,' said Mum, entirely unbothered.

I can happily report that the thermometer is no longer there.

So we had our cheerful, funny moments, which kept me alive. But there was always something that could render me sad in a split second; some reminder of my old life that the 'hall of mirrors' had taken away.

You could see it too in others around me. My friend Danny, one of the most injured in the Edgware Road train bombing, suffered bad nightmares afterwards. He remembered seeing the bomber pull the cord that detonated the rucksack. He was still angry, and who could possibly blame him, but he had a fatherly attitude towards me. If I'd been out with friends in the evening, I'd come back from The Red Lion with a Chinese and offer him a spring roll to appease him.

'What time d'you call this?' he'd say, like a surrogate dad.

'Do you remember last night?' he'd ask the next morning.

I always said 'no', whether I did or not, just to make him laugh. Making the best of things. What else could you do?

Everything is different now, I'd think. This body isn't mine any more. It's somebody else's. Yet it *was* mine and I was going to have to learn to live with it.

4

The Wright Stuff

I'm a true cockney – born 30 September 1972 at St Bartholomew's Hospital, within the sound of Bow bells in east London. I'm also a mistake, or a 'surprise', as my mum put it more tactfully – ten years younger than my sister, Tracey, and seven years junior to my brother, Grant. Breaking the news to them, Mum and Dad tried as diplomatically as they could to offset the shock.

'We've got good news and bad news,' they announced. 'The good news is that you're going to have a little baby brother or sister. The bad news is that we're going to have to get rid of the dog.' As a tactic it went down badly. My sister thought the whole thing was disgusting and my brother was outraged.

'I don't want a baby,' he argued. 'Why can't we just keep the dog?'

So I came into this world as a poor dog substitute who endeared herself even less to the family by regarding sleep as a waste of time. Mum, in desperation, went to the GP, who advised a little tot of whisky in my bottle. Apparently I slept better, but every time I burped I smelt of scotch. However, at some point they must have relented towards me because I have wonderful memories of a very happy childhood. I was sociable, chatty and independent from a very young age, apparently as far back as my attendance at Mrs West's play group in Edgware. Mrs West smoked about eighty fags a day and would plonk us on her lap to join her in her personal cloud of smoke and fag ash. I loved it there.

It's where I met one of my lifelong friends, Lianne, and we discovered we were fellow tomboys. We were pretty cute, in the street-smart sense, even then. We worked out that if we sat in the paddling pool and drenched our dresses we'd be allowed to raid the dressing-up box. Dodgy brown corduroy trousers and other manly attire was the prize, which, although they smelt pretty bad, of boys and cigarettes, suited us much better than dresses.

In Lianne's dad's shed we formed a group of girls called the 'Red Hand Gang', after a TV programme, and her Chopper bike and my old Grifter were our 'wheels'. We went to Brownie camp together, supposedly in the wilds but actually at a farm up the road, so that Brown Owl could call my mum for a box of matches when someone had forgotten them.

It was at nursery when I made my first appearance in the *Times* – the *Edgware & Mill Hill Times*. A dressing-up competition was being held for the best-dressed mini-Queen as part of the celebrations for the Royal Jubilee of 1977. My Auntie Jeannie, who was a dab hand at dress-making, rose to the occasion. She was my dad's brother's wife, a remarkable woman who introduced me, aged eight, to the 'snowball', the cocktail of choice in that era if you liked ominously thick egg-yellow stuff called advocaat. To a recycled Little Bo Peep costume she added a floor-length cloak made of blue velvet, decorated at the edges with cotton wool and black dots made with a felt-tip pen. The majestic effect was finished with a crown covered in fruit gums for precious gems that to me truly looked like she'd nicked the entire crown jewels.

I won. Perhaps it was the awakening of my competitive streak, although I suspect it was there all along.

Furthering my education, I went to Broadfields Infants' School, to be taught in reception by the lovely Mrs Rudolph, who smelt like strawberry milkshakes. I was the type of child who made friends easily and flung herself into things, not always to the delight of the teachers. I remember one particular glockenspiel incident.

Not being divinely musical, but longing to join in, I was given the responsibility of hammering at the school's wooden glockenspiel – a sort-of big-time xylophone – at a special concert to which our parents were invited. This was a big deal, and I'd learned my part devotedly. At the appointed moment I was given a shove by Mrs Lewis, the music teacher, and began my assault on the instrument. My dad was a passionate DIY-er and I modelled myself on him hammering some innocent piece of wood in the garage.

While this performance was going on, I could feel a tug on my skirt. I ignored it, except for wrenching myself out of its grip with sudden lurches. This greatly added to the effect. The audience was transfixed. Finally the music came to an end and reluctantly I hung up my hammers. An explosion of applause rang out – from my mum. Turning round, I saw Mrs Lewis holding her head in her hands.

You could say enthusiasm marked much of my school career. At home I had a very pink bedroom (my mum's doing) with Wham! and Tears for Fears posters on the wall, and I loved watching *Tiswas*, *It's a Knockout*, *The Battle of the Planets* and *Crackerjack* on television. Anything anarchic and action-packed I loved. My brother used to force me to watch *Lassie* too because he knew it would make me and Tracey cry. I had to lock myself in the toilet to escape him when it came on.

I remember odd incidents from the rough and tumble of family life, like Grant and me both being rushed to A&E on different occasions. Him because he fell in a cesspit and me because Graham Bell knocked me off a bench reaching for a bottle of ketchup and I cut my head open.

But otherwise it's a happy blur of playing out with my friends, like Lianne and Claire, family parties and loads and loads of Sindy toys. I had a Sindy horse, Sindy caravan, Sindy buggy, Sindy wardrobe. I even used to insist that when I had a dog, male or female, it would be called Sindy.

My brother objected as furiously as he could.

'I'm not shouting "Sindy" in the middle of the park,' he cried, horrified by what his mates would say.

'Why not?' I demanded, completely unable to see what was wrong with it.

Anyway, the dog – when it arrived as a little fluffball, after years of begging – was called, as a compromise, Cindy with a C.

I think Mum had resisted the arrival of another dog for such a long time because three kids can be hard enough to manage but, more than that, she had a devotion to cleaning. She used to hoover at 7 a.m. She had this incredible skill that allowed her to strip beds with you still in them. On a Saturday morning she'd come into our rooms, rip off the pillowcases, get us to lift our bums up, so she could take off the bottom sheets, and then, making us hold one corner of the duvet, she stripped off the cover as well. We'd carry on lying there, on the mattress, as she swept out again. I don't know why she didn't just shout at us to get up, but she didn't.

We also had a 'best' room, with a green velour sofa and purple carpet that was absolutely spotless at all times. We never used to sit in it as a family; we all used to pile into the TV room instead. Dad had extended the house, his DIY hammering working to great effect by then, and it was a decent size for us all to spread out. Even so, there was nowhere to put the pool table I'd been given for my eleventh birthday, so Mum heroically let me use her best room. 'Be Very Careful,' she warned me. And, knowing she meant business, I was Very Careful.

My brother and I got on fantastically well. Tracey, being that little bit older, was more of a mystery to me. I mainly remember her crying all the time, over boys – from a Paul McCartney lookalike (that really pleased her) to a heart surgeon's son (a popular choice with my mum). She wasn't overly fond of a baby sister invading her room, either. I was never allowed in when she was playing Monopoly with friends and I got the drift that I was a major nuisance.

My brother was the complete opposite. He used to play with me all the time, although he drew the line when he had to babysit in public. Mum would go off to work or shopping and leave both Grant and Tracey with strict instructions to look after me. Without fail there'd be a big row as soon as she left.

'I'm not looking after her,' one would announce.

'Well, I'm not looking after her. I looked after her last time.'

'You didn't look after her last time. I looked after her.'

'Oh God–' looking round '–where the hell is she?'

All the time this was going on, say, on the way to the local bus stop, I'd been aimlessly wandering away and then they had to break off the ruck to run round the streets and find me. I don't remember ever being scared on my own. I liked my independence. And, in a funny way, it was a vision of what would happen later on, when I looked after my Nanny Thompson, my mum's mum, who had Alzheimer's and would hop on buses going anywhere if we didn't catch her in time.

My mum used her very best efforts to get me to be a proper girly girl but I always resisted. There are pictures of me on my tenth birthday standing next to a Smarties cake in a red Spanish flamenco skirt and a comb with a red flower in my hair. The look on my face is faintly thunderous. The prelude to the picture had been a fierce argument with me saying I would never wear that stupid comb thing and my mum saying oh yes I would. She obviously prevailed for a very short time before I found an excuse or played some raucous game, which made it surplus to requirements.

I was much happier pottering around in the garage with Dad, fascinated by all his tools and devices. I especially admired his vice, and he would blithely let me have a go with all kinds of gadgets that could take your fingers off in an instant. I loved them. Unfortunately for us, when Mum was standing at the kitchen sink she had a great view of the garage interior from the window. Our activities were regularly interrupted by furious banging on the glass and wild gesticulations as Mum sussed I was about to do myself a mortal injury.

'S'all right,' Dad would say, and wave at her airily, the sound of a power drill filling the air while Mum had a meltdown on the spot. He had great faith in my powers of self-preservation.

He was pretty handy with jobs. He had a few of them. As well as being a plumber he was also a black cab driver, same as Lianne's dad, Keith. That became relevant on those occasions when a bunch of school friends and I – probably no more than ten or eleven years old – would sneak on the tube to central London, which we were expressly forbidden to do. Lianne and I would have a completely miserable time, desperately hoping we wouldn't see a black cab that might contain one of our dads. So it wasn't a great idea to go down Oxford Street, which we always did, where there were thousands of them. We were constantly ducking into doorways.

A cab ride with Dad was much more entertaining, especially when we went down to our static caravan in Clacton-on-Sea. It had been in a right state when he bought it, but with his DIY skills he'd done it up and Mum had christened it 'Martine', with a wooden plaque to match. We stayed on a campsite called 'Rosebank', which had a club, a games arcade and a swimming pool.

On the way down, he'd let me change gear while he was driving (only seven years before I'd be allowed to take my driving test) and on arrival he'd go straight to the bar.

He always brought a mate along for him and I had one for me, usually Lianne or Claire. We'd have complete freedom to roam. Dad would only see us when we needed change for the slot machines.

'Here ya,' he'd say generously, doling out some coins. 'And have a couple of pounds for a cola and a packet of crisps. Want some cockles?' It was bliss.

Later that evening, he and his mate would return to the caravan, somewhat merrily, and make us a sandwich, turning Frank Sinatra up to max. This would result in people knocking on the door, complaining. He dealt with them effectively, if not tactfully. 'It's only ten o' clock,' he'd say, and slam the door shut. One night, a furious resident wrenched the door open so hard that Dad wondered if he'd broken it. He hadn't though, so Dad took a screwdriver to it himself and then reported the neighbour for the damage.

He had other ingenious ways of dealing with the moaners, one that included me. He'd get us girls to stay up until about one o'clock in the morning, when the whole campsite was quiet and everyone asleep, and then give us a lump of bread, crumbled into pieces.

'Right, take this and throw it onto that caravan's roof,' he'd instruct, pointing to the den of our complainer. Off we'd go, giggling uncontrollably. Sure enough, next morning our neighbour could be heard complaining bitterly about the gulls that had landed and thumped about on his roof since the crack of dawn.

I also remember playing Russian roulette with eggs, boiled and otherwise, which you smashed against the side of your head. Boiled was fine, they stayed intact. Fresh eggs covered you in gloop, all dripping down your face and over your hair. Proper laughs we had there every time.

I was very chatty. A teacher at my junior school, Mr Mason, called me 'Mighty Mouth', which didn't offend me at all. In fact, I pretty much loved all my teachers, until I was confronted with the wrath of Mrs Benson. She was tough. So tough that when one boy was caught stealing things from the coat pockets of other children, she tied his hands together with string and hung a huge sign round his neck saying 'thief' that he had to wear all day. He couldn't eat his school dinner without help because of his day-long handcuffing. He didn't steal again, though.

I was in her bad books from the start because she'd hated my brother who'd gone before me. Mum was always up the school having massive rucks with Mrs Benson because Grant, being dyslexic, had trouble in class. But if I wasn't clever I was astute, and I spoke up. Never stopped speaking up, really. Eventually she came to quite like me for my enthusiasm.

My final accolade at junior school, before moving up to secondary, was to win the 'Wally of the Week' cup, during our last school journey to Yorkshire. On this particular day we were canoeing on a lake and, as usual, I was in the company of Lianne, who was paddling alongside me. I was rather annoyed to discover, furthermore, that she was paddling faster than I was. As unofficial team leader, and being highly competitive, I found this hard to take.

'You're going faster than me. What are you doing?' I demanded crossly, getting redder and redder in the face with effort.

'I'm not doing anything,' she said with genuine innocence.

'Well, I should be going faster than you.'

'Well, I can't help that.'

'It must be your boat,' I concluded. 'Let's swap.'

'I don't think that's a good idea,' she protested, in vain.

'You stay there and I'll put one leg in your boat . . .'

As I did so, both boats drifted apart and I performed an impromptu underwater routine, much to everyone's hilarity. No one was going to beat me to the Wally of the Week cup after that.

I attacked things with gusto. Sport, choir, school plays – including one memorable rendition of a dwarf in our version of *Snow White*. I wasn't fazed by much, so advancement to senior school held no terrors. Orange Hill, as it was called, merged and converted to Mill Hill County High while I was there. It's still there, with a big signed photo of me on its wall (which makes my nephew Felix and niece Matilda, who go there, very proud). Who would have guessed at the time?

Apart from the dreaded cross-country running I adored sport and was pretty good at it. Badminton, netball, tennis and particularly hockey. I was school player of the year three times running. Any sport where you can play centre-forward and whack a hard ball at a target was always going to suit someone like me.

But most of all I loved my schoolmates. Still do. Lianne, Claire, Michelle, Tara, Shirley – we've got a Whatsapp group called 'MissingMyGirlies'. Obviously we've taken different paths: marriage, children, responsibilities etc., but we've got a shared history that goes back a long way. We weren't really rowdy but we enjoyed a laugh and supported each other to the hilt. I like to think we were all quite astute and savvy about staying out of real trouble but this did not always come to pass.

Various escapades come to mind. The school had expanded very suddenly, and there wasn't enough room for everyone to have lunch in the building. This meant that second and third years, of which I was one, had to be chucked out on the streets every lunchtime. This was fantastic, we thought, hanging about next to the ice cream van eating a healthy lunch of sweets called Nerds and Space Dust and waiting for someone to have a fight (usually Claire).

Obviously some parents were not terribly happy with this arrangement and the local newspaper got to hear about it. They sent reporters down to talk to us about how 'awful' it was and lined us up for a photo – which we obviously loved. It was snowing at the time, which made the story even more compelling. We posed and, as the camera clicked, I fell over, sprawling on the floor in front of everyone. That picture made the front of the *Edgware & Mill Hill Times* too.

Then there was the time that our friend Ricky was having an overnight sixteenth birthday party in his massive barn in Watford. We all ended up having a food fight and, quite rightly, were chucked out by his family. We didn't dare go home so, after trying to kip down in a derelict 'haunted' house up the road, followed by the local golf course (uncomfortable and cold), we decided to go round to Tara's house, although she wasn't with us at the time. I have a distinct memory of Claire up a drainpipe, trying to break in.

Ridiculous things. One Halloween we thought we'd break into Highgate Cemetery to give ourselves a fright around Charles Dickens's gravestone. Although only one of us got over; I was stuck halfway up the wall and the rest gave up. And anyway, Charles Dickens is buried in Westminster Abbey.

As we got older we found ourselves involved in the usual random adventures. Some of the girls met a bunch of friends from Burnley when they were holidaying one year in Spain, and to this day I reckon I got my travel bug from weekend coach trips to Lancashire to visit them.

Inevitably, bad things happened too. Tara's mum,

Eileen, who we all knew, died of cancer when Tara was sixteen. Lianne was staying over at my place the night before and Mum had to tell us both in the morning. My dear nan had died, and that was very sad, but this was a real tragedy. We had the day off school and spent it crying with Tara at her house with the curtains drawn.

The funeral was a very emotional day. All our mums were there and, in the evening, I went with my friends to a flat belonging to Claire's sister, Kelly. She had a baby and a place of her own. Somehow alcohol and marijuana was produced, none of which we could handle, and when we heard a loud bang on the door we all immediately thought it was the police. It was worse. It was Claire's mum shouting, 'Let me in!' at the top of her voice. The wrath of Rita was famous. There was a major jostle for the baby, all of us figuring that Rita wouldn't do anything terrible to endanger a tiny child. Lianne and I legged it for the balcony and were seriously debating whether it would be safer to jump two storeys than stick around to face Rita. We thought better of it and we were all sent home in disgrace.

You can see why Tracey would be furious that I'd be allowed freedoms she'd never had at my age. Mum always said, 'That's because Martine's very mature for her age,' which, of course, infuriated Tracey all the more.

Even so, I think I *was* mature. Wiser, in a way, than my years, partly because I had older siblings and partly because it was obvious that Mum and Dad were not really happy together. They argued for years. I can see now that they were both stubborn and couldn't communicate. Mum was quite proud and wanted things done in their own proper way. Dad wanted to go out and have fun. But at the time, as a kid, it just made me sad that they seemed to be shouting at one another so often. I used to take Cindy out for walks to avoid it.

It reached the point where, as a teenager, I dreaded my dad being at home when my mum was there, fearing an argument when the two of them were together. Divorce was on the cards quite a lot. Going right back to primary school days, I can remember a school journey to Swanage when both Lianne and I were in tears because she had just discovered her parents were divorcing. I thought mine would too. The teacher, Mrs Watts, kindly tried to console us with the promise we'd be made prefects the next year. With a bit of theatrical gulping on my part, the promise largely succeeded.

I didn't think any more of the episode until Mum went to an open evening and came back looking shocked and upset. The next morning in the car on the way to school she had a serious conversation with me.

'You didn't tell me you were upset about me and your dad arguing; Mrs Watts told me.'

I tried to fob it off. 'Yeah, but it was just that Lianne was upset and I sort of joined in.'

'Well, your dad and I have had a chat and we're going to give it another go.'

I remember to this day the sinking feeling this gave me. I was thinking, I don't want you to give it another go. I want you to get a divorce so that everyone can be happier. But I was only nine. I couldn't actually say that.

It happened in the end, when I was fourteen. Some argument had flared up as usual and Mum said, 'That's it, I want a divorce.'

Dad asked me my opinion, and whether they should give it another go.

I had the maturity by then to tell him: 'No, Dad, I don't want you to give it another go. I want you and Mum to get a divorce. I can't take any more. You won't be on your own. I'll be there. We'll all be there.'

Things were so much better after that. Tracey and Grant had already left home and Mum and I moved to a house in Mill Hill, which we hated from day one because we didn't realise the M1 ran along the bottom of the garden. But at least there was no more arguing. Dad moved into a bungalow and eventually married, by coincidence, Maureen II.

We're a very happy family now. Funnily enough, deep down, we always were. But sometimes human beings just aren't made to live side by side.

At the close of my school days I had to decide what to do. Something in the business line, I thought. I found a year-long diploma course in advertising in Watford, which was perfect, plus there was a great student bar. I'd race there and back in my new lime-green Mini with black 'go faster' stripes that I'd bought from a district nurse. I was pristine. On arrival. But not destined to stay that way.

I had my first brush with the law in that Mini. Dashing to the corner shop in it, loaded with school pals, seemed an innocent thing to do. But when we came out with our purchases I noticed some van had blocked us in.

'Oi,' I started to say, and then noticed it was a police van.

'Is this your car?' asked a police officer.

'Yes, er . . . officer,' I said, trying my best to be polite.

'Do you know what speed you were doing?'

'No, er . . . officer.'

He told me an outrageous figure, although I can't remember now exactly what it was.

'Do you live round here?'

'Yeah, just over there.'

He was beginning to relent.

'My colleague and I were just saying that your car looks like something out of a Scalextric set.'

He had relented. I drove home with elaborate caution.

As well as old school friends there were new pals to be made on my diploma course, and we'd frequently go out together to the big club in Watford, formerly called Bailey's (when my mum and dad went there) but at that time going through its 'Kudos' phase. I knew it pretty well from nights out during my A-Level year with schoolmates, all in our wraparound tops, flared trousers and fake IDs, coming home at 3 a.m., then trying not to fall asleep over our desks the next day.

Diploma gained, I was ready for the world of work. Nearly. Lianne had just come back from a summer with Camp America where she'd met a girl called Juliette and now they were going to Thailand.

'Mum and Dad,' I said, 'I'm going away to Thailand for three months.'

'Oh no you're not,' they said. 'People will put drugs in your suitcase. You'll get attacked on a beach. It's far too long. You'll run out of money. We'll never see you again . . .' Etc.

I went to Thailand. Until that point my most far-flung holiday had been a week with my schoolmates in Tenerife (with big permed hair, if I remember rightly). Thailand was a game-changer. Now it's a regular holiday destination but in the early 1990s parts of it were tremendously remote. That's where we went. Day-long treks over unmade roads with ten-foot craters. Sleeping with hill tribes, including their pigs. Staying in the chief's hut, where you were served with boiled eggs and opium. That was an interesting mix, especially with pigs sharing the accommodation.

I realised I had a bug for travelling. When I came home, to a job of reclaiming used videotape for the BBC (unbelievably boring but at least you could watch *Neighbours* while doing it), it was only a matter of time before I went away again. This time it was just Juliette and I on a working tour of the Far East and the Antipodes. It was an eight-month adventure to Malaysia, Singapore, Thailand again (especially the beautiful island Ko Pha Ngan, before it became famous for its full moon parties), Australia, New Zealand, Indonesia … and a farewell week in Bangkok.

This was before the era of mobile phones and email, so Mum and Dad were gripped with terror a lot of the time, as they heard absolutely nothing from me. But it was party time for us, on next-to-no money, with top-ups of work in between. We lived where we could. We shared a flat with twenty-five other people in Coogee Bay, Australia, when we had a job selling promotional pens in Sydney. We lived in our hired Datsun in the car park of a hostel in Queenstown, New Zealand. Our diet consisted of mashed potatoes and cheese sauce, plus noodles on special occasions and wine by the box.

Naturally we had to do a bungee jump. My mum only found out about this when she received a package in the post containing a video and strict instructions: '1. Don't watch this on your own. 2. Don't be holding a hot cup of coffee. 3. I'm absolutely fine.'

The footage opened with a pair of trussed-up feet and the off-camera sound of someone crying, 'Mum, Mum, help me, Mum.' Me, obviously. There was then a long section of a male voice shouting, 'Three, two, one … BUNGEE!' followed by a close-up of me screaming, 'No!'

Eventually, out of sheer shame, I flung myself into the abyss and screamed all the way down.

The next day we returned to collect the offending souvenir video and the women at the reception seemed fascinated to meet me.

'Oh, we thought your video was so hilarious, with all that crying, so we're using it in our promotion.'

I tried to get it for free. She wouldn't have it. But I did make it clear that I hadn't been crying, I'd just been terrified and emotional.

So, how do you follow a holiday of a lifetime like that? I didn't want to go to work yet, so I went to university. Mum had found me a joint Communications and Psychology degree course at the University of East London and I enrolled literally off the plane after a twenty-hour flight in a state of such grunge that the tutors at the induction spoke exclusively to my sister, as though I wasn't there.

Ideally I'd have lived in the East End for those three years. Instead I lived in a house in north London with my six mates from school. Many people might have moved, but the pull of friendship was more important, and I drove round the dreaded North Circular in a sporty mint-green Fiesta. I made friends on the course with a great girl called Harriet, or 'Harri', and she often let me stay with her, which was easier on the hangovers. By the second year I'd stay over regularly with my latest boyfriend, Jonathan, who lived with seven girls in Bow and had parents with a posh house in Henley. We went out for quite a while; the latest in a line of interesting boys that had begun with Scott Marchbanks, who thrilled me because his family owned a hardware shop and we were allowed to deliver coal to the neighbours on a little trolley. I was five at the time.

But the love affair with Jonathan came to grief when he failed to mention, even though I was living with him, that he'd got a job in Switzerland. I was in a rut anyway. I wasn't enjoying my job. I was selling stationery in Boreham Wood, which would be enough to depress anybody. I wondered what I'd be good at. My CV was varied, to say the least:

Coal woman, aged seven (see above).

Milkmaid, aged fourteen, when I was allowed to help my dad's mate, Ron the milkman, on a Saturday morning, which he began with a tot of whisky before setting off on the float. I loved it – the old dears paying me 16p in 2p coins for their goldtop and Ron shouting 'Martini!' up and down the street when he wanted me.

Member of a focus group for £25 a day – great money but a complete farce because we pretended to be whatever they wanted at the time: 'mother of two children into travelling and golf' or 'eighteen-year-old student studying A-Levels'. You name it we were it. I do hope the companies that based their products on our suggestions found it useful.

M&S saleswoman – a job I returned to with frequency

in the holidays. I loved that too, minus the time we got held up at gunpoint in Mill Hill.

'Don't get anywhere near me, lady!' the bloke shouted, waving the gun at me.

'I'm not getting anywhere near you,' I shouted back, and proved it by diving under a counter. Luckily he panicked and ran off.

Breakfast waitress and chambermaid at Trust House Forte at Scratchwood Services. Great job, because I'd be finished by lunchtime and could sit in the family room watching *Neighbours* with a wafer biscuit and cup of tea. That's where I met the laundry boy, David, who became my first proper boyfriend.

However, none of these excursions into the world of work was a long-term prospect for a graduate. So I looked around and eventually came up with a sales job at a company called Mercer Grey, an IT recruitment firm with offices in Piccadilly, just opposite the Ritz. That's where I met my fabulous friends Sarah Jones and Alex Ogden, who was my boss.

By now I was sharing a house in Barnes with my uni friend Harri and her friend Sarah. It was dangerously close to the local pub. So local that it wasn't unknown for me to turn up there in my pyjamas or take a turn serving behind the bar. But that way of life, and indeed that wonderful career, was coming to an end. The turn of the century was dawning and we were persuaded that when 1999 became 2000 all the computers in the world would break down. I thought I'd get out first and, anyway, my job was changing from sales, which I loved, to 'IT Recruitment Consultant'. That wasn't for me, nor my work colleague Claire. I gave my notice not long before Christmas 1999.

I had no idea what I was going to do . . . and then came Emma. It's like a handbrake turn in my life story and, whatever subsequently happened to me, this was a tragedy with no happy ending.

A lovely friend called Joe, who I'd nicknamed my adopted little brother, had left Mercer Grey a few months before me. We stayed in touch and, as luck would have it, he was going to be in my favourite place over the coming Christmas and New Year. Claire and I only had to hear the words, 'Come to Thailand,' and we were practically packing my bag as he spoke. 'You'll meet an old schoolfriend of mine,' he said. 'Great girl called Emma.'

Emma, by ridiculous coincidence, was the daughter of my sister's boss at the BBC. He'd been my boss for a while too, poor man. So we knew of each other before we actually met and, when we did, in some remote bungalow by the sea on an island in the Far East, we hit it off immediately. It turned out she too had been a kind of mediator in her family when her mum and dad divorced. Maybe that had a bearing on our instant liking for one another, but we used to spend hours in our hammocks, just talking. She called me her soul mate, although, because she was dyslexic, I was known as her 'solemate'.

We had great fun, as well as our heart-to-hearts, although typically I also managed a trip to hospital after crashing into a wall on a moped. But the most significant thing was the decision we took on New Year's Eve. I had no job back home, and Emma and Joe were going to take a chance on finding a job and living in Australia. Why didn't I join them? Emma and I would get a flat together in Sydney. Why not? Everything seemed a whirlwind after that.

I flew home to tell Mum, Dad and the family. Everything seemed wonderful. My whole life was about to be transformed. I started to gather up my things, most of which were in Golders Green, where I'd been sharing a house with Michelle and her brother Anthony before I'd gone to Thailand. I condensed everything back at Mum's for a few weeks while I sorted my visa and wondered how the hell to get everything I needed in one suitcase.

It was a thrilling countdown. On the day before I was due to fly, unbeknown to me, Tracey was growing concerned by activity in her boss's office. This was, of course, Emma's dad. People were going in and out looking terribly distressed. He was in there on the phone.

Seriously worried, she asked one of his closest colleagues what was going on. 'Please tell me what's happening. My sister's due to meet Emma in Australia the day after tomorrow.'

It was bad news.

Tracey called Mum, who came to find me, still packing.

She said she didn't know any more than what she was about to tell me, but something had happened to Emma. Something was very, very wrong but no one knew any details.

It made no sense to me. Emma had just gone to visit her ex-boyfriend and his family in New Zealand, to celebrate her birthday. That wasn't exactly a dangerous location. She was staying in a really safe place with people she knew. The word came back that she'd had 'an accident'. I was going crazy with worry. In the end Tracey came back with as much information as she had.

It was the most random of accidents. In the middle of her birthday party Emma hadn't felt well and had gone upstairs to lie down for a while. One of the family went up to see how she was and Emma decided she was well enough to join in again. On the way down one of them slipped and they both fell all the way down the stairs together. Emma hit her head on a flagstone at the bottom. She was in hospital, in a coma; her mum and dad flying over to be with her.

I still have the vivid memory of being at Mum's, in the bath, crying and crying and being in a desperate dilemma about what to do. Should I go? Should I stay? What if she survived and I wasn't there? I knew what I had to do. The packing suddenly wasn't so important. It didn't really matter what I took with me. The vital thing was to go. Harri, my old university friend, was in Sydney. I arranged that I'd go and stay with her when I landed. As soon as I arrived I called Mum. 'It's OK, I'm here safely,' I started to say.

'Martine, I need to stop you,' Mum interrupted. 'Emma died last night.'

I can't think of Emma to this day without being desperately sad. Such a waste. Her poor family. All they could do was take her home for the funeral. I debated about staying in Australia but my heart in the adventure was completely gone. I just wanted to go home again. I was there forty-eight hours in total. I must be one of the few people in the UK who's been to Sydney for a weekend.

At least I could help in one way: I could bring all her things back home for her mum and dad. She was very arty and a great photographer, so there were loads and loads of photos. I started to look at them during a stopover in Japan and had a long cry. The funeral was just devastating too. Meeting her younger siblings who knew all about me because she'd written home umpteen times about her 'solemate'. Awful.

She's with me still, in a way. There's a picture on my fridge of the pair of us on a swing, backs to camera on a deserted beach gazing out to a beautiful sea. That's how I remember her, and she continues to give me strength. She didn't survive her tragedy like I did mine. I'm the lucky one. She reminds me how lucky I am.

Naturally, I didn't feel particularly fortunate just then. Missing Emma with no job in the depths of the English winter was miserable, but Alex, my old boss, was working on another IT project. She knew what had happened to me and how desperately sad I was. She told me to come and join her. The trusty old distraction technique. It was good to be doing something again and the work certainly had its fun moments. It's hard to believe that I once shared a desk with Pippa Middleton (her uncle was a board member of the parent company) and a cardboard cut-out of Jude Law. But I did.

It was carnage, since the job pretty much involved going to dot-com parties all over London during the internet boom of the early noughties and being tremendously sociable. Part of our day's work was to give away gifts and gadgets that IT professionals, basically men in those days, would appreciate – like a Smeg fridge full of beer or a shot glass chess set. It was a mad whirl.

And then I met this guy, Nick. I remember where and when. It was my friend Sarah Jones's birthday, 4 July, at the Duke of Devonshire pub in Kensal Rise. It was her party. I'd introduced her to her new boyfriend Darren a few months before and Nick was one of his friends. We got talking. I told him my name was Sonia, just for a laugh, and watched his face drop about a foot.

'What's the matter?' I asked, mystified.

'Nothing, nothing,' he said, trying to brush it off, but still looking horrified. I found out later. His ex-girlfriend who'd treated him miserably was called, of all things, Sonia.

Still, apart from that glitch we 'got on well': my

euphemism for snogging. So well, in fact, that he wondered where I lived. Ah, I sensed a problem. Because I'd promised a sofa for the night to Joe, as in my friend/little brother Joe, who happens to be model-looks gorgeous. Nick's face fell another foot when I told him that and then disappeared into the night with this Adonis.

I called him the next day to apologise and, fortunately, within no time we were a couple. I can't deny there were rocky times. We were so very different, plus geographically separated, with him in Brighton and me most definitely in London. Not long before 7/7 we'd broken up because I was in a general state of dissatisfaction. Big mistake. I missed him. He wasn't the problem. It was me. I was restless.

In the spring of 2005 we got back together. He had this house in Brighton that he was doing up and I was living in a flat in Crouch End, but we tried to see each other as much as we could. My new high-powered marketing job, based at Tower Hill, was OK, although the daily commute could have been easier. Lots of tube journeys and changing trains, depending on which line was running properly. The secret was to be flexible but, as far as possible, never ever take the dodgy Circle line. That line was an absolute nightmare.

5

Come Fly With Me

Now I know, but I didn't then. Not for years. Now I can look at the huge work of art on our wall – a stark black-and-white version of London, created by Nick – and I can start to understand what he went through. It's in front of my eyes: layer upon layer upon layer of photographs so that the city is both familiar and desperately strange. At first sight it looks like a jumble of half-seen people, places and movement. But when you look closely there's the sign to Aldgate tube station, the entrance to The Royal London Hospital, the bedlam of streets, footsteps and traffic lights, buses and taxis, the roofs of City monuments, the blank glass face of tower blocks.

That's how London felt to him after the bombing. He felt alienated and angry, yet he betrayed none of this to me while I was in hospital and then rehab. Lost in my own little bubble, I admit I barely noticed. I had battles in my own head and with my own body to fight and, looking back, it's shocking how self-centred it made me.

He thought only about making me feel better, and sometimes I realise that I thought only about me feeling better too. When I went through those 'Why me?' moments, I sometimes I forgot to say to the man I loved: 'How are you?'

He wasn't well. He wasn't fine. And yet he was there, almost every night, beside me. He abandoned his home in Brighton and was living in my flat in Crouch End to be nearer to me. That meant every day he was confronted with me, my stuff, my old life . . . my shoes. It tore him to pieces. He had a job he didn't particularly enjoy that heaped extra stress on him. He had no car at the time so he had to travel to work by bus and tube on the very Piccadilly line on which twenty-six people died in the 7/7 attacks. At the end of the day, when he was exhausted, he took another set of buses to and from the hospital to see me.

He'd come through the door. I'd smile and say, 'Hello, babe,' and then he's ask about me. He must have been exhausted. I just didn't see it. I only know now, not because he ever moaned to me about how terrible it had been, but because he dug out his old diary to help with the writing of this book. Typically he did it for me.

He talked to me, apparently, when I was in the coma, willing me to get better, and then he just listened to lots of Radiohead and tried to keep going. This, as he tells it, is how it was.

'It kind of felt like my duty to keep going. I couldn't not. I couldn't leave her. I couldn't face her and say, "This is too much for me. I'm going down to Brighton to get on with my life. See you later." I couldn't have coped with that. But subsequently it was incredibly tough.

'I think I was very, very angry during the whole year that followed. Just going to work on the Piccadilly line was bad enough. We knew people who'd been injured on that train and the horror they'd endured. Sometimes I'd get on a bus or tube and see someone who looked a bit like the bombers. I'd just get up and walk off. Once I said, "I'm really sorry, mate, it's nothing to do with you." It was a simple case of visual association.

'After work I'd take the train and bus to Waterloo and go to Roehampton, where Martine was by then in rehab. I'd stay with her until about 9.30 p.m. and then come back the same way every evening. I was drinking about four pints of Stella every night, or anything else I could lay my hands on, just to get me through. I was almost an alcoholic – and still so angry.

'The lowest point was the night of the 'folk rage' incident. That's how it has gone down in history. It was about February time and Martine had been in hospital for seven months by now. One of my friends, Tim, invited me to come and see a folk musician we both really like called Roy Harper at the 100 Club. I had begun to think I was feeling better but, in actual fact, I'd been bottling things up. As well as Martine, things were going badly at work – rushing round, not getting feedback, pretty soul-destroying. Not getting enough sleep. Being an alcoholic.

'So, we went out this Friday night and I was really tired. I'd drunk three or four pints of Guinness in the bar and then we went down to listen to Roy. He's an incredible singer-songwriter; one of the best this country has had – deep, romantic and meaningful. I just went a bit loopy and wanted him to sing about Martine. I started to tell people about her and I lost it. The audience was a serious bunch of music fans and they told me to shut up. I would never try and hit anybody or anything, but I was shouting back at them: "Shut up yourself. Don't you know what's happened?"

'I remember the look of fear on Tim's face. Then I lost my memory. Next thing I know I'm being carried out. The air sobered me up a bit. Tim was in shock but I said I'd be fine and we separated. I tried to find my way home but I went back into being in a stupor. Then I was suddenly in a tube station, an old one, somewhere like Mornington Crescent, not knowing where I was or what I was doing. I was stumbling about in a state. I've got a feeling a police car came along and they probably took pity on me rather than slamming me in a cell because I woke up at home, back at Martine's flat.

'I went back to work the next day, distinctly hungover. I said: "Sorry, I'm a bit late," and then became very upset. Even my boss's steely exterior broke a little bit. She realised I wasn't better. I left the job the following month and started out trying to be a photographer instead.

'I don't really know where my rage was targeted. I think it would be a bit thin to say I was angry at the bombers. I take a while to consider things. I like to think about philosophy, current affairs, religion and things like that. I worked out that I was really angry at the fact I couldn't get anything back for Martine. There was no retribution. The bombers were dead. Her legs were gone. I was also angry at people because people just kind of carry on doing their thing. Nobody really gives a crap. This massive thing is happening and I just have to deal with it. Deal with London. I've always seen London as this huge, living entity, and while this was going on it felt hostile.

'I wrote a poem on the bus one night, probably quite drunk, on my way back from visiting Martine. It began:

> Sometimes you have to revel in shit
> When the good is disguised
> By the smog of bad feeling
> No chink of gleaming white light here is in such a place
> Just argument and arrogance
> The City needs this rebirth.

'I do find myself back in 'good London' again now. A few weeks ago I walked from Paddington to Islington, a really lovely walk, thinking and looking at the people, and it was nice again. But I could never, ever, live there again.

'It was bad, to be honest, right up to the Olympics and Paralympics in 2012. I'm still moving towards the person I've always wanted to be.'

Nick kept all this from me while he was by my bedside. I'm not necessarily someone who appreciates the finer points of poetry. I was looking for a bucket to throw up in, not a rhyming couplet, for most of my hospital stay. This wasn't exactly the romance he'd signed up for: a girlfriend in hospital for a year, with no legs, a mad family, no money, no job and what future?

I was in hospital for thirteen months altogether. Rebuilt from a wreck to a living, breathing, walking, part-computerised human being. Now it was time to leave my hospital nest and that abnormal 'normality'. I was thrilled and I was scared at the same time. Would I be able to say goodbye to my friends and walk out of Queen Mary's without crying for hours? Answer to that one, no.

I'd been allowed out of hospital at weekends when my sister would come and pick me up after her work. Mum slept on the sofa-bed to give Nick and I a bedroom of our own but, to be honest, a kiss and cuddle on the sofa was the full range of my seductive activities. Basically, I was knackered.

I think I knew we were going to be a committed couple. I don't know whether there was a flash of light. More likely it just dawned on me that he was always going to be there. Maybe I took advantage of him, maybe I took him for granted, especially the day I said, 'Goodbye, I'm going to South Africa now for six weeks.'

It wasn't quite that stark, but close. It was my social worker at Roehampton who started it. She told me about flying scholarships for the disabled and I thought, Ooh, I might try for that. So I did. There was a two-stage interview at RAF Cranwell in Lincolnshire and I was with thirty or forty people who had all been through something similarly traumatic to my own experience.

On arrival we were greeted by a man with a typically wonderful handlebar moustache, who told us that we had to prove we could independently get in and out of a small plane in the event of an emergency.

A challenge always does it for me. When it was my turn, he had barely said 'go' when I charged over to the plane, got up on the wing, in the cockpit and out again. (I didn't have my legs on at the time.) 'My God,' he spluttered, 'that's the quickest time I've ever seen.'

I hadn't long been out of Roehampton when the decision came that I was on the course. I was going to learn to fly. Not just the two-day event at Goodwood, but the full scholarship. Six weeks in South Africa. Brilliant! But oh, my God, was I ready for this?

To leave Nick, the family, my friends, my future, still up

in the air to go and be *up in the air* . . . I could see the illogic. I could feel the slight bewilderment of everyone around me. What does she want to do that for? But I knew why. There were so many things I could no longer do in the way I'd done them before – walking being one of them. But here was the opportunity to do something astoundingly new and wonderful – to fly. It was about rebuilding a new me who wouldn't have to look back all the time with a sense of loss. This was going to be bloody great.

Even so, it was daunting and, to make it more challenging, Heathrow decided to have a bomb scare on the day of my departure. I thought, No, surely, this couldn't happen to me twice. Mum, Dad and Nick all came to the airport and they were surely thinking the same thing, but we said our significant goodbyes. I'd barely been apart from them for six hours over the past year, let alone six weeks, and there I was, gone. I was really going to learn to fly a plane in the beautiful blue skies over Africa.

OK, no one told me that it rained in South Africa in August. That was my first mistake. It didn't just rain, it poured down. Visions of cocktails on a sun-drenched veranda, after a few aerial stunts before lunchtime, had to be hastily revised. Plus I was so, so homesick. My fellow trainees were lovely: Judith (our mum figure), Kathy, a young 'English rose', who had survived a back tumour, and Paul, a farmer, paralysed from the waist down following a road accident. Nice people, but I had really underestimated how much I would miss home.

I missed Nick and our physical closeness. I missed my family. I missed my home comforts. But then I'd shake myself and remember that I was living a dream – being up there in the clouds, looking down on a world I nearly hadn't rejoined after my 'accident' (as I still called it) only thirteen months previously. The first time I took the controls of the plane was amazing, although I did wonder whether I was doing it because I actually wanted to or whether it was to prove to myself, and others, that I *could* do it. Either way I was bloody well going to do it.

Such was the pace of our training I barely had time to wear my legs. Maybe I didn't quite have the confidence either. The first time I did wear them I fell arse over elbow in the dining room. The next time, in the rain, admittedly, I fell over again. It reached the point where it became an everyday occurrence. People glanced at me and then just carried on with whatever they were doing.

The opportunities for leaving the training base were few and far between, given our hectic schedule, but Judith and I decided to take a rainy day to explore the local hotspots. We hadn't gone far down the road in our van when a sign announced: 'SLOW DOWN: Cheese World'.

'Did you see that?' I said to our driver, pointing and laughing. 'That's hilarious.'

'That's where we're going,' he replied, seriously.

That was the hotspot. Anyway, I bought some chillies and a toy Tyrannosaurus Rex for my nephew, trying to radiate an enthusiasm I didn't feel.

Rainwear became an urgent necessity. First I borrowed an old yellow Batfink coat that made me look like ET, which I replaced with a new navy blue mac as soon as I could. This gave me confidence and so, sauntering along the road with Judith one day, I was lured by a guy into his shoe shop. Clearly I was destined to disappoint him.

'I don't really have a need for shoes,' I said, pulling up my jeans to show him my metal legs.

Poor bloke, he looked a little horrified for a moment, and then said, 'What about a skirt?'

Full points for positive thinking. I didn't buy a skirt.

There were nights out too, most memorably at the 'Snorting Grunter', a nightclub named after a fish. Despite the name it was certainly a popular spot. Roughly in order of occurrence, I had a few dodgy wines, watched a local version of the Chippendales (the bit where they ripped off their boxer shorts looked quite painful to me), got swung round the dance floor, spotted a Freddie Mercury lookalike, switched to Peroni, admired the full-length beard of a guy about four feet tall, switched to cider and lemon and left at 3 a.m. If I was trying to reclaim 'normal life', this probably wasn't it.

One sunny afternoon I was up in the plane with my instructor, Nick, practising 'circuits', as we called them – flying the plane round and round over the airfield. Nick did one as a demonstration, then handed me the controls and said, 'Go on, then. What comes next?'

Considering I have a three-second memory like a gold-fish, I said, 'How the hell do I know?'

Then he said we'd attempt a few landings. What? This was seriously nervy stuff and, as I grappled with the controls and terror, he said I was apparently scared of the ground.

'I'm in a plane, going at eighty-five miles an hour and heading into the landing strip – of course I'm bloody scared of the ground!' I replied. But I did it. One unaided landing. It felt wonderful, marvellous. And the buzz lasted all night.

That was one day. The next was different. Even the other instructors were surprised that Nick was insisting we go up in such terrible conditions. Flying in such desperate turbulence was the scariest thing I've ever done – up there with bungee jumping or falling into the longest rapid in the southern hemisphere, both of which I'd done in my mad past. The wind was forty knots that day, the G-force felt like a roller coaster, the plane was spinning, the horizon was going round and round and, the worst of it was, you couldn't shut your eyes. At one point it really felt like I was freefalling and going to die. When it was over I staggered to my room feeling thoroughly sick.

But I went up again the next day – and this time saw four rainbows.

It was only later I realised how like life it was. You never knew what was coming. The good, bad, terrible, beautiful, and you just had to face them all the same.

But for all I seemed to be coping with life on the 'outside', sometimes I was sideswiped by a completely random incident. In a shopping centre one day I saw the sign on a disabled toilet door. 'Paraplegic' it said, uncompromisingly. Another time, an elderly African woman noticed me and asked bluntly: 'What's wrong with you? Are you a paraplegic?'

Leaving the Snorting Grunter one evening, I was stopped by a young woman who said she was from London. She added, 'Oh, it's so good seeing people like you out.'

I felt like punching her.

'Look love,' I said, 'I was like you a year ago except I was unlucky enough to have my legs blown off.'

She looked distraught and apologised. Perhaps I should have controlled my temper. She was copping for a lot of feelings that were building up in me. But it got to me. Being at the nightclub probably got to me too. I'd look around the dance floor and it hurt to remember that I was like that once. I'd watch the dancers covertly and wonder how they would cope with all I'd been through.

I know why the hurt stung so much. This was me in the outside world – not a cushy existence supported by lovely people who wished me well. The real world was the world that didn't give a damn what had happened to me; it had too many problems of its own. It made me vulnerable and sad. The 'why was it me?' thoughts would drift back into my head like smoke. I couldn't stop them.

I didn't admire myself for thinking them, but I knew they was still there.

But I couldn't dwell on it. This was no soft option. Flying school wasn't a case of, 'Ah, you're disabled, you don't have to do this.' It was serious stuff. It's the best thing I could possibly have done. It wasn't really the flying that mattered. It was about getting my independence back.

Sometimes I didn't really want it *that* much, though. Like the day we went to Port Elizabeth and I had to land at a 'proper' international airport. Towers, concrete runway, air traffic control, the lot. I can remember what I was repeatedly thinking: Oh, my God! It was hellishly hot in my flying suit and, being in a little Cherokee plane with the air coming through, I couldn't hear what air traffic control was saying.

There was a noise though. A distinct roaring.

'What's that?' I asked my instructor.

'Oh, that will be the Boeing 747 behind you,' he said.

Still, there was good news. My taste buds, wrecked by the accident and the drugs regime that followed, were beginning to come back. The bad news: now I knew the wine was terrible.

There was further good news. We would be allowed a day off to visit a local game reserve, so Judith and I decided we would go to their tourist information office at the nearest major town, Port Alfred, to buy the tickets. To keep things simple we would catch the bus and take our wheelchairs. Prosthetic legs – given my strike rate of falls – would be best left back at base.

The first problem we encountered was that the bus station was on one side of town and the tourist office on the other. No problem, we were on a mission. There were no dropped kerbs, so we had to wheel ourselves along the roads, one side of Port Alfred to the other, stopping at red lights and doing hand signals. I appeared to be going faster than Judith, even though she had an electric chair and I was puffing and pushing my manual version.

At one point I turned around to see she had a traffic jam of about a dozen cars behind her. It was probably the biggest traffic jam the town had ever seen. I couldn't stop laughing.

Obviously people couldn't help staring. At the bus station, on our way back, we faced the usual 'Oh, what happened to you?' questions. I wondered if I should be more inventive. Maybe I should have told people I was a lion tamer who put her legs, rather than her head, in the beast's mouth and the act had gone slightly wrong.

Priscilla, who ran the flying school kitchen, had a daughter who worked for the traffic police in Port Alfred. She said, 'I bet my daughter rings up and says there was a huge traffic jam in town caused by two ladies in wheelchairs,' and we all fell about again.

We went on safari to the game reserve and it was amazing. We saw water buffalo, giraffes, zebras,

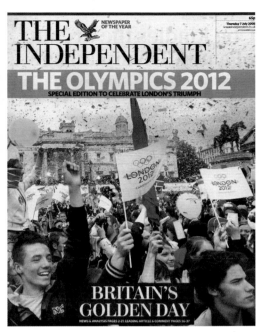

7 July 2005 – this was the newspaper I was reading before the bomb exploded. I kept thinking that as a Londoner I needed to get tickets to this huge event.

8 July 2005 – 24 hours later and London and its people were in a very different place. My family were still searching for me at this stage.

Wreckage of Aldgate tube – I was sitting where the huge hole is in the side of the carriage. A reminder of how lucky I was.

Rolling back the years – my sister Tracey, aged 11, my brother Grant, aged 8, and me, aged 1.

Happy days at Mrs West's playgroup.

Mum and me – still insisting on putting bows in my hair!

Me and my very special Nanny Thompson.

Dad (Papa) and me on holiday, Portugal 1983.

The 1990s – first girlie Spanish holiday away.

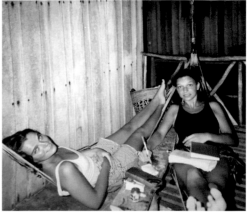

Thailand – chilling in a hammock with Lianne.

G'day mate! Sydney harbour, 1992.

One, two, three, bungee! Queenstown,
New Zealand.

Christmas Day 1999, Thailand, with my 'sole
mate' Emma (to the right of me).

Any excuse for a party – thirtieth birthday, surrounded by friends.

My Michey – great friend and godmother.

Graduation, 1996, University of East London.

Viva Las Vegas – work achievement weekend with the IT job board.

At Joanne (Nick's sister) and Simon's wedding, Burgh Island, 2014.

Miss Hasu Patel and the dream team at Harrison Ward, Royal London Hospital.

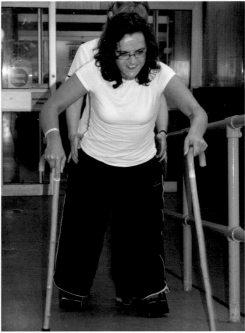

My lovely Maggie helping me walk on 'rockers'.

Working on my core strength.

D-Day – standing up for the first time on 'real' legs.

What we were made to do in the name of occupational therapy!

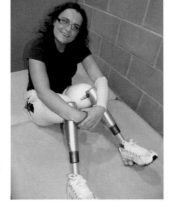

Finally, going home after a year in hospital.

One of my first visits to a pub, with Alex and Sarah.

Come fly with me. South Africa, 2006.

Wipeout. Skiing, Andorra, 2007.

Ten thousand feet up and strapped to a stuntman from the new Batman film.

Just married, May 2008 – memories we will treasure forever.

Two very special guests – Maggie Uden (Walker) and Miss Hasu Patel.

Dancing with Dad.

Friends and family who really made the day.

NCT gang – great friends all waiting to drop big babies!

Oscar, our little monkey, our most beautiful and precious gift.

Ukraine, September 2011 – continental cup.

28 August 2012 – we made it!

Emma and me in opening ceremony outfits. Ali G, here we come!

roebucks, warthogs, elephants, lions – sightings only slightly dimmed by pouring rain and the fact we were desperate for the loo after four hours in the truck. Kath jumped out in a hurry, but her crutches slipped and she fell, whacking her head against the door of the car. As she cried in pain, I just had to sit there until someone could help me move.

It was a reminder: a disability can really be disabling. At times like this it hit me that I wasn't like other people. Unfortunately, in my new life, I had my limitations.

But sometimes people placed limitations on me that I fiercely felt I didn't deserve. Right at the start of the flying escapade I'd been asked about my injuries. I innocently mentioned the minor, incidental fact that I'd suffered a hairline fracture of the skull, among the other much more serious things. Oh, God, how I wished I'd never said a word about it.

At the mere mention of a head injury everything stalled. I could fly but, without a battery of psychological tests and the approval of doctors, I would never be able to fly solo, and that was the whole point of the exercise – to give people with a disability the opportunity to rebuild confidence by doing something as amazing as a solo flight.

I tried and tried. I did tests; you wouldn't believe the tests.

'Could you tell me,' the examiner said, in the sort of sing-song voice reception teachers deploy, 'what year this is?'

'What?' I thought he was going to ask me about Einstein's theory of relativity or something.

Amazingly I knew the date, my name, who the prime minister was and what a pig looked like.

Presumably I passed that test.

It didn't make any difference. I even rang Hasu in London to help. She tried too. But the rules were the rules and ultimately I had to give up on that particular ambition. I expected to be furious and distraught and, although I was for a while, it didn't last. Just flying through storms and rainbows, meeting people, causing traffic jams in Port Alfred, missing home, talking, laughing, socialising, maybe they were enough.

One evening, towards the end of my three-week stay, a Scotsman called Ian asked me again what happened on The Day. Normally I'd bat the question away, as it was too raw and too recent to delve backwards. But there was a last-day-of-term feeling in the air and I told him properly this time. Tears started pouring down his face as I explained what had happened and how upset I felt about what Mum and Dad went through when I was missing. I did well to keep back the tears myself.

Sometimes I still couldn't believe what I'd been through. And sometimes my mum and dad couldn't believe it either. 'Oh no,' they said. 'No, no, no,' when I told them about the parachute jump.

It was Maggie, my physiotherapist at Roehampton, as usual, who came up with the opportunity. She was doing a sponsored skydive for the Flying Scholarships for the Disabled charity, which had just sent me to South Africa, so of course I had to have a go too. It would be a small way of saying thanks. And it would be another way to prove to myself that, yes, there were things I couldn't do any more, but so what? This was something fabulous that I *could* do, and not in the least dependent on having a pair of legs.

We converged – with the family, as usual – on a field in Oxford for the great day. My instructor was a man with a huge handlebar moustache and a spectacular tan. He said he'd just come back from America.

'Oh, whereabouts?' I asked politely, being a fan of tans myself.

'Well, all over,' he said. 'I'm a stuntman in the new *Batman* film.'

'Wow.'

He was quite dishy for an older man. My mum took a definite little fancy to him. She kept touching his arm and saying, 'You will take care of my daughter, won't you?'

All right, Mum. That's enough.

I say it was lovely day but I was also pooing myself. Obviously it was a tandem dive and I was safely strapped to this guy who'd done countless jumps and defeated loads of *Batman* villains, but it was still terrifying. The plane climbed and climbed.

'Are we there yet?' I kept asking, like a kid in the back of a car.

'No, we're only at three thousand feet. We don't jump out until ten thousand.'

Oh, my God. A good proportion of my heart and soul was wishing I'd never done anything as stupid as this, but then the door opens, you feel the rush of air, you're shoved to the ledge, your adrenalin's off the scale, and the next thing you know you're hurtling towards the earth, screaming.

I felt I couldn't breathe because of the pressure. I was totally disoriented. The G-force was terrific; my face felt like it was about to fly off. Everything I'd learned in the thirty-minute training session beforehand went out the window. I only started to enjoy it when the parachute opened and we began to float serenely to the ground. I went from roaring in fear to yelling, 'This is amazing!'

My family heard me before they saw me appear through the clouds. My instructor said that had never happened to him in all his years of flying.

So, a new life was beginning. I was positive but for one thing: I was worried about money. It hadn't mattered in hospital when surviving was more important. Then walking. Then flying. But coming home to Nick, my family, my new life . . . I suddenly thought about it on the plane home. What the hell were we going to do for money? I wouldn't be leading a normal life. I knew in my heart of hearts I didn't want to go back to work in marketing. I'd need wheelchairs. I'd need an adapted house. My mum had told me how much it would cost just to flatten her drive. £9,000. Oh, my God.

At least the housing situation was clear. While I'd been away, Nick had found a place in Hertfordshire. I'd still been in rehab when that process started. My social worker had told me that due to our exceptional circumstances – camping at Mum's and not having a place of our own – we could apply to our local council for somewhere to live temporarily. So we applied to Barnet Council, where Mum lived, and Hemel Hempstead, where my sister lived. After all that had happened I didn't want to live in London any more.

We filled in umpteen forms and a letter came back. Basically it said: 'Good luck, there's millions of people ahead of you'. Mum and Dad were furious. I was desperately disappointed. Then I had an idea. I wrote a seven-page letter to Tessa Jowell, the MP who was at the time the head of the 7/7 Assistance Unit. I explained that Mum was living on a sofa bed in her own living room so Nick and I could have a bedroom because we had nowhere else to live; that I'd been an international marketing manager but was now thrown into a world of disability. I told it like it was. Her PA, Alex, phoned me immediately and said, 'Yes, we'll help.'

That happened literally as I was climbing aboard the plane to South Africa, so the house-hunting was up to Nick. He viewed a few scuzzy council flats in Hemel that smelt of cat's pee, and then said he found this one nice place in Berkhamsted. What he didn't tell me was there was a ruddy great wheelchair lift coming up through the floor.

That threw me when I first saw it. My first thought was, What the hell's that? My second was that it would be a constant reminder of the fact I was disabled. My heart sank. But it was light; it was clean. Actually it was a nice space. There was Dad lining the walls, my brother doing the bathroom and Nick (not really his thing) tiling the kitchen. I privately thought that he'd been wrestling with the same tiles for the entire six weeks I was away, but I didn't say anything. And so that's where we lived. Our first house together. I get quite a warm feeling when I think about the place. It healed us.

I suspect Nick doesn't have such a warm feeling, though, because we had dodgy neighbours who used to play music till 3 a.m. and it drove him quietly mad. Didn't bother me. Perhaps we argued about it; we have regular rucks. But we get strength from each other even though we work at different speeds. I drive him nuts flying along at 90 mph. He drives me nuts. We're a classic example of the tortoise and the hare. But we communicate and I think we've got a strength other couples don't have.

We've had a lot of stuff to get though. I used to think, airily, Yeah, me and Nick, we can get though anything. That's basically right, but I've come to learn that when something traumatic happens to you it happens to your family too. There were things that Nick had suffered while I was in hospital that I didn't come to understand for a long, long time.

'I wish we had a normal life,' he'll sometimes say, wistfully.

'What do you think a normal life is, babe?' I'll answer.

So we had somewhere to live in the short term and that was great. But the fight for criminal injuries compensation had only just begun. For some reason I was made spokeswoman for those injured in 7/7 and their families. I don't know why I say 'for some reason'. I know full well the reason: I've got a big mouth!

A number of top legal firms offered their services free of charge for the victims. They explained how the Criminal Injuries Compensation Authority worked and the numbers horrified me. The injustice was stinging. They had decreed that loss of one leg was worth £55,000, two legs £110,000. But for more than one injury you were actually penalised. My arm injury was worth £12,000 but I'd only receive £6,000, as my legs had been blown off too. It was deemed a 'second injury' and so paid at fifty per cent. My burst eardrums? I don't remember now. Maybe the full amount was £2,000 and I only received a third. I was being penalised for being more injured.

It wasn't just me I was worried about. It was all of us who had been injured in our various ways and all the bereaved families I had come to know. Those poor people who had said goodbye to husbands, wives, children, mothers, fathers one morning and had never seen them again. Some, in the instant of those explosions, had become single-parent families with no income. Even in the depths of their shock and grieving they would have to go to work. How would they afford the childcare?

The more I thought about it the more outraged I became, until one of the senior partners of the legal firm, Irwin Mitchell, asked me to have a one-to-one chat with Attorney General Lord Goldsmith about it. From that meeting came an invitation to speak to a group of his parliamentary colleagues from the House of Lords, about the issue of compensation to families and the value of the *pro bono* helpline, set up straight after 7/7 to put families in touch with vital legal services for free. I was very nervous about doing it. I felt really quite scared. But I knew I had to go through with it, to speak on behalf of those who had suffered and were still suffering, not just from injury, not just bereavement, but also the ongoing mental anguish of that day.

I took Dad with me. Partly for practical reasons, as I still needed help getting in and out of cabs with my wheelchair, and I suppose I just needed the confidence of someone I loved being with me. I also took him because he and Mum had been great beneficiaries of the *pro bono* helpline right at the beginning, when I was still in hospital.

They'd been thrown into this world where their

daughter had just been blown up by a terrorist bomb and lost two legs. Who's prepared for that? And who has the headspace to think about money and the future when they're just worried about their child staying alive? I wanted to tell the lords and ladies I'd be addressing at the presentation how valuable the help had been. I wanted to make Dad proud, too, so he could go home to Mum that night and say, 'You should have seen her!'

We were summoned to a glass building next to the Houses of Parliament. It was a hot day; the sun was streaming through the windows and heating up the room like a greenhouse. It was stifling. But I refused a chair and stood alone in front of all these lords, dames, lawyers, and whatever else they were, leaning on my two sticks for support.

I wanted to speak my mind. I'd been told I could. Yes, it was to talk about the benefits of the *pro bono* system and how it helped all the families, but I'd also been explicitly told: 'All the questions you've been asking, you can now personally ask the Attorney General himself.'

So I did.

- Why hasn't there been a public inquiry into the 7/7 bombings?
- We know the security services had information about the bombers before it happened, so do we not need an inquiry to learn from it?
- How are the victims to be compensated?

- Did they know the compensation ceiling was £500,000? That was set in 1996. Shouldn't that figure be updated?
- Why are you penalised the more injured you are?
- How did they work out the figures for compensation?
- Bereaved families were being paid just £11,000. Didn't they think that was ridiculous?
- Did victims have to pay tax on the figure?

Did those in government understand this was not just about money? It was about all the victims having to live that day over and over again. Through paperwork, official administration, the media, or just other people's day-to-day reactions. Injuries were not just physical; they were mental, emotional. Unfortunately I was on the tube that day and I can never, ever, escape from the aftermath of that. Every anniversary will be a reminder that plunges me back to the moment my life changed.

I spoke from the heart and told them what the day had done to me and my family. I told them I'd lost both my legs and that no one and nothing could have prepared me or my family for what came next. There was no survival guide to turn to. While I was lying unconscious in hospital, my family had no motivation or energy to do anything except be there for me.

That's why the *pro bono* system worked. It was a friendly, helpful, knowledgeable voice on the phone that explained a system none of us knew existed. Why would we? None of us expected we'd ever need to delve so deeply into criminal injuries compensation. To us, the lawyers who donated their time were vital go-betweens with a world we didn't understand.

But . . . there was a 'but'.

On behalf of those who had lost the family breadwinner, I told them I couldn't believe that the compensation was just £11,000. For someone with young children who would now have to find a job and not be there for their five- and seven-year-old children who'd just lost a dad . . . I could feel myself getting massively het up. The sun was still pouring into the room – it was boiling hot in there – but I remembered the people I'd been meeting. They were really raw, really angry, and it was my duty to speak on their behalf.

I'm glad I said my piece. We never did get a public inquiry, though. And the compensation payments are still pegged to their 1996 limits. So I didn't make a difference. I hope one day that changes because the fact remains if you're blown up by a suicide bomber, resulting in life-changing injuries and trauma, you receive far less compensation than if you're run over by a truck. In that case, it's the truck driver's fault or the company he drives for. We couldn't go after the bombers; they were dead. They had chosen to die, trying to take as many of us with them as they could, killing fifty-two and injuring 700.

We were financially punished for being victims of a terrible atrocity instead of a road traffic accident. Seemed mad to me. It still does.

*

My old job was being held open for me, which was amazingly kind but it wasn't as simple as that. For a start there was the financial element and then there was the general loveliness of the people I used to work with. Kathy, my former boss, had sent me a text: 'We're all so proud of you. You're really so special. Please, please, please get yourself better and come back to work.'

I wanted to try for her, I really did. I just didn't know whether I was psychologically strong enough to go back to my former life when so much had changed. I arrived on my first day back by taxi, my wheelchair folded in the back. I went through the entrance on wheels, the same entrance I'd always run through in the morning. All my work colleagues and friends were there, just the same. Except I wasn't.

I couldn't walk to the printer any more. I couldn't jump up and fetch a cup of coffee. Everywhere I looked there were memories of how I used to do things and how I was now doing them in an 'awful' way. That's what I thought. It was 'awful'.

I'd been there a couple of weeks when I went to see Kathy. She looked at me and said, 'I know why you're in here.' I started crying.

'Don't be silly,' she said. 'We knew this would be hard.'

She was right. It was too hard. Somehow I'd have to move on.

Hardest of all was going back to my flat in Crouch End, the one I'd rushed out from, running late that morning on

7 July 2005. It had been frozen in time and it was nearly two years since that date before I finally found the courage to go back through the front door. The first thing that confronted me was the staircase I used to run up two steps at a time. I remembered that old independent life, when my biggest worry was whether I'd have time to get to Londis before it shut after pub closing.

This time Dad had to manhandle my wheelchair to the top of the stairs and I had to climb them on my bum. One at a time. I reached the top and broke down in tears. Those bridesmaid shoes, still in their Next bag, behind the sofa . . . I wondered if I was brave enough to open them up. I did, but had to close the lid. I was crying again.

I was sorting out clothes that didn't fit me any more; flip-flops I'd never need again. There were my old shoes. I used to go clubbing, for God's sake, in high heels. I've still got some of those shoes. They're in the loft. I don't know why; maybe there's too many memories attached to them. Hey, they're nice shoes.

I tried to sift through my stuff but it was like digging around in a graveyard. That old life was dead and buried. I just wanted to get out of the place. I didn't want to be there any more. It was another part of the old life. It had to go.

6

Love and Marriage

On my wedding day I imagined I'd walk down the aisle in a beautiful dress on the arm of my beaming father. No walking stick, no wheelchair, just a radiant bride floating through clouds of flowers and the happy faces of the people she loved towards her husband-to-be, smiling at the altar. The Mills and Boon vision cracked a bit after what happened to me.

I couldn't walk any distance aid-free without the real risk of falling over with spectacular inelegance. Nick would not be smiling at the altar; he'd probably be as nervous as hell and worried about dropping the ring. I hadn't worn a dress, beautiful or otherwise, since before 7/7. And, crucially, Nick hadn't actually asked me to be his wife.

Our life together was lovely but admittedly chaotic. I

was still trying to fit as much as possible into every day to rediscover who I was. He was, deep down, still reeling from everything he'd been through and trying to set up his own photography business. And then there was rediscovering each other through our sex life. I had so many other challenges going on, it was one of the last things on my mind.

The physical side of our relationship hadn't been a huge facet in our lives while we were staying at Mum's, on those weekend breaks from hospital. We were sleeping in her bedroom for a start, littered with framed photos of me as a baby and bunches of flowers everywhere. It didn't really set the scene for a night of hot passion. And, anyway, Mum was just through the wall on the sofa bed.

But later, in our own bed, in our own room, in our own house, we had to confront the issue. It would just simmer otherwise and settle into a serious problem. The solution turned out to be holidays. We went away for weekends together to places like the Peak District, or even further afield to Spain where a generous stranger called Eileen, who'd read my story, lent us her villa for a week. These gestures from people we didn't know were incredible. Having known the worst of humanity once in my life, I'd experience the best over and over again.

Eventually I found the courage to ask Nick a question that had been nagging at me: 'Do you still find me attractive?'

It mattered so much because, in my mind, what

remained of my legs was awful to look at. They were damaged not just from the initial injuries but also very scarred from repeated operations.

Nick looked at me dumbfounded. 'Don't be stupid,' he said. 'I love you because I love *you*, not your legs.'

And that was that. It worked. Someone loving you to your bones is a pretty good aphrodisiac. That and a good bottle of wine.

We were a team, Nick and I, throwing ourselves into What Happened Next. We couldn't quite believe the turn our new life was taking. The invitations and opportunities were off the scale: a skiing holiday, a safari, a royal summons to Prince Charles's residence at Highgrove in Gloucestershire.

They were all unforgettable; the Highgrove event for more reasons than one. This was a highly emotional occasion, a reception for 7/7 survivors and the families of those who had lost someone on the day. It was deeply moving to be reunited with people like Kiera, Thelma, Philip and Andy, all of whom had been injured in that Aldgate carriage with me, except Philip who had been on the Piccadilly line train. Our affection for each other ran deep. We'd been together in The Royal London's Harrison Ward while we were trying to overcome the mental and physical trauma of our injuries.

As often tends to happen, my feelings got the better of me. At one point I was standing on a terrace, looking out over the most beautiful gardens, when I spied Philip through the crowd – not difficult when he's six foot five. I felt inspired to rush over and say hello, probably because I had a clear vision of the last time we'd talked. He'd lost a leg in the bombing and, like me, had struggled to make sense of it. Yet we'd held hands at The Royal London, just before I left for Roehampton, and I'd promised him with absolute determination that we would both get through what had happened to us to one day live life to the full again. And look at us now, mixing it with royalty.

I went over, full-tilt on my prosthetic legs, to give him a hug. I arrived at high speed and, with only one leg between us, our hug turned into a dangerous totter. Inevitably we toppled over and crashed to the ground. Everyone gaped in horror. Of course, I couldn't get up independently, and had to lay there until someone pulled me upright again. It was highly embarrassing. My new sunglasses flew across the patio and the lenses got scratched, which should have annoyed me no end. But I laughed and thanked God that Princes Charles had yet to make his entrance. I was spared making a Wright royal prat of myself.

His Royal Highness arrived later and had clearly been briefed, as he asked me about learning to fly. I tried to speak intelligently to him but it was gradually dawning on me that I could have chosen my wardrobe more wisely for the occasion. I'd gone for an elegant low-cut top, which would be fine if you were looking someone in the eye. But from a seated position in a wheelchair the angles were rather unfortunate. I had a horrible feeling I was giving an eyeful to the future king of England.

Prince Charles appeared entirely unbothered. I'm sure many worse things have happened on royal visits. I could have relaxed and forgotten all about it, except one of my mates had to come up with the line: 'Nice one, Martine, You've just flashed your charlies at Charlie.'

Life was settling down a bit, but still I had no job, no real day-to-day focus. I didn't have agonising flashbacks or the nightmares that afflict some people after a trauma, but I knew I wasn't entirely healed either. All sorts of ideas were suggested to me. One that appealed most was simply going away on holiday to Andalucía in a six-some – Nick and me, Alex and Rob, Sarah and her boyfriend Darren.

I still felt guilty for missing Alex and Rob's wedding. Maybe it would lay that ghost as well as being my first major holiday with mates since 7/7. It was two years ago now. Time very much to move on. My plan was to play cards, drink a hell of a lot of tequila and have one big party.

We'd hired a car there, which seemed sensible for dashing to the shops when the supplies ran low. Nick was always trying to get me out in it somewhere. Being artistic, he wanted to share a sunset or mountain view or something with me. Being relaxed, I wanted to see an ice-cold drink and have a laugh with my mates.

'Come on, let's go for a drive,' he'd say.

'No, let's stay here and play cards.'

'No, let's go. There's this beautiful ravine ...'

'No, I think it's really unfair you keep asking because the car only seats five and there's six of us.'

'No, I just mean you and me.'

'No, we can't just leave all the others.'

So the conversation would go on until, in the end, I thought: Oh, I suppose I'm going to have to give in to him at some point. I knew he wanted to take photographs. I couldn't think of anything more boring, but I roused myself. The girls checked the fridge and asked us to bring back butter, bread and vodka from the shop.

One of them said, suspiciously, 'Why is there a bottle of champagne in the fridge?' The boys all started talking at once. Except Nick, who fled the room.

In the car, he was fumbling around with the CD player. That ancient tune 'Love and Marriage' came on. 'Oh, I like that,' I said, singing along. I didn't have a thought in my head except that it was a sunny day and if we hurried up we could get a few games of cards in before supper. Finally we reached the salt lakes Nick was so keen on and, I must admit, they were very beautiful.

'I'm going to get out and take some photos,' he said. 'Why don't you get out too?'

'Nah, I can't be bothered,' I said, thinking of the palaver with the wheelchair.

'No, come on. It's beautiful,' he insisted.

'Oh, God, all right,' I said grudgingly.

So we got the chair out and I sat myself down, resigned to a tedious wait while he took his beloved photos. But he wasn't taking pictures. He was there in front of me, kneeling.

'Martine,' he said holding my hand. 'Will you marry me?'

I'd had no idea. No inkling at all. All the blinding hints and I'd been completely oblivious. He'd been planning to do it for days and days, getting more and more panicked and finally confiding in the blokes, who just told him to bloody well get on with it.

I immediately burst into tears. And said yes. Of course I said yes. I'd sort of presumed we were engaged once before, hadn't I, in my drug-addled state in hospital. Now it was for real and he was putting a ring on my finger. I mean literally. He had a ring with him that he'd secretly smuggled all the way to Spain. Naturally I didn't like it.

'Oh, that's a nice ring,' I said woodenly, lying.

'I knew you'd say that,' he said, with a grin. 'Don't worry, I got it from John Lewis. We can take it back.' Proof that I was marrying a man who understood me.

I was engaged. All I remember after that is excitement. I was in the car calling Mum and Dad and there was lots of screaming and crying down the phone. Dad already knew because, being a great traditionalist, he wouldn't have been happy unless Nick had asked him first.

Somehow, in all the frenzy, I remembered the shopping and we arrived back to find the rest of the gang looking at us expectantly (boys) and suspiciously (girls). They knew something was up; they just didn't know what. I played it incredibly cool to begin with.

'Hiya, guys. We've got the bread, we've got the butter, we've got the vodka and . . . *we've got engaged!*' I screamed. They screamed. The champagne cork popped and I woke up the next morning with a massive hangover. But that night, when everyone had gone to bed, Nick and I lay in each other's arms out on the veranda, overlooking a picturesque valley under the stars, and I remember to this day exactly what I was thinking: it was the first time I really felt like 'me' again.

Above all I wanted two things from my wedding day: to walk down the aisle on my new legs and to have a massive great party. I knew it would be an emotional day because of all I'd put my family through while I was in hospital. This was to help make it up to them. I'd been desperately sad to miss Alex and Rob's wedding, so this was my payback time. It was a chance to have a re-run when everything was fine. Symbolically it was going to be a big day.

I planned it meticulously, which included a rehearsal at one of my rehab sessions in Roehampton, when I went back to refit my legs. I grabbed one of the doctors to stand in as my dad and another one – one of the top amputee surgeons in Europe – was drafted in as the vicar, holding a flowerpot as a Bible. I found it difficult to go through the whole ceremony without stumbling, but Maggie kept hauling me to my feet and promising me I'd be fine on the day.

The wedding dress I chose would be the first dress I'd worn since before 7/7. It had to be perfect, but the search was pretty daunting. Some of the bridal shops I visited were a bit fazed by a bride-to-be with two metal legs who inevitably became hot and bothered after a few minutes of wrestling in the changing room with stick, legs and wheelchair – and that's before a multi-layered dress was added to the mix. I began to think I'd be looking for a long time. Then I found the perfect one in, of all places, Tring. My new home town.

The next quest was for shoes. Mum and I went to Watford and I couldn't deny a small sense of heartbreak every time we walked into a shop and saw racks of gorgeous, glamorous silky pumps that the fashion industry reserves for weddings. I was in my chair wearing long trousers so, when we said I was looking for wedding shoes, the assistants naturally assumed I'd be wanting the 'Cinderella' look.

I don't think twice about it now, but back in those days it still hurt to lift up my trouser legs and reveal the metal rods underneath. It always led to an awkward pause and endless displays of trainers and plimsoles instead. Few women want to wear Skechers on their wedding day but, after a long, long search, that's what I found. Gold Skechers. I'm not knocking them. They were quite feminine, glitzy, matched my cream-coloured dress and, above all, I could walk in them. That dream of walking, really walking, down the aisle was becoming a reality.

But only if I could get Nick into a church. He had a bad experience of church as a kid and doesn't really like organised religion, being more a kind of spiritual pagan/jedi mix. He'd have infinitely preferred to have held a ceremony in a field, probably sitting on hay bales instead of pews. Fortunately his dad rings the bells at a church in Great Missenden, in the Chiltern Hills, and I was able to lure him round to the idea: 'Wouldn't it be great to get married at your dad's church?' The vicar, called Rosie, wasn't too vicar-ish either, and had a big thing for nature, so in the end he was quite comfortable with it.

I'd planned our wedding day so meticulously that, when it arrived, I expected a sense of calm bliss to descend on me. Nothing had gone wrong in the lead-up. My beautiful wedding dress had been delivered the night before by the dressmaker, Sarah, who, as a special gift, had sewn a Swarovski crystal onto every single button that lined the back. Michelle, my bridesmaid, was staying overnight to help me in the morning. Nick was probably not going to jilt me at the altar. The flowers were gorgeous. My lovely friend Michelle and my niece Lissy would be wonderful bridesmaids, and my other niece, Matilda, was a picturesque little flower girl. I drifted off to sleep in expectation but no panic.

Next morning it was, of course, madness and chaos.

Mum and the hair and make-up artist converged on the doorstep, along with my two excited nieces. Michelle was helping me dress and, above all, paranoia was gripping the representatives of both *Hello!* magazine and *News of the World*, to whom we'd given exclusive rights to the wedding pictures. They were convinced that other media organisations were going to try and steal a glimpse of their own. Their rampant fears lent a James Bond-like spy vibe to the whole proceedings.

When I was dressed and ready, I descended to the ground floor in our house lift like a musical star being lowered onto the stage. I should have had dry ice swirling around me when I emerged, legs on, nervous, excited. Dad was there to meet me and, as everyone started to leave for the church, we had a few chill-out moments on our own in the kitchen.

'You do know how much I love you and how proud I am, don't you?' he said, holding my hand.

We both had tears in our eyes.

'Dad, I've just spend an hour-and-a-half having my make-up done, please don't make me cry.'

He felt in his pocket for a hip flask to ward off the threatening tears. We stood there together, a peaceful moment, having a quick swig of brandy each before the drama began.

Outside my fabulous Rolls Royce Phantom was waiting, complete with chauffeur – a gift from one of my former bosses, Bill – closely followed in convoy by two huge black Range Rovers belonging to the *Hello!* and *News of the World* teams, while overhead whirled a helicopter they were convinced belonged to a rival media outlet, threatening their exclusive coverage. When another Range Rover began to follow us they thought that could be 'the enemy' too. It was turning into a car chase.

When I arrived at the church I was shielded by a line of white umbrellas – in case of unwanted invaders with cameras – and then I stood at the door waiting to go in with my bridesmaid making final adjustments to the veil, my gold shoes sparkling beneath the dress and my dad having one last swig before the off.

But everything faded to a distant blur the moment the organ music began and I had to concentrate like I'd never concentrated before on getting down that aisle safely. I clutched my bouquet of cream roses and set off. The congregation burst into applause. Dad was smiling and holding firm. My sister had given Dad's wife Maureen explicit instructions to check his pockets just before he left home that morning. We knew he had one hip flask on him but he'd actually managed to smuggle three on board. But all I cared about was getting alongside Nick safely. I tried not to look around to see who was there in case it distracted me from the task of walking, and by avoiding eye contact I hoped I wouldn't burst into tears. Essentially we'd all gathered under one roof: my dearest friends, family, Nick's family and the people who had given me so much care, like Maggie and Hasu, to make this moment happen.

I'd joked beforehand that those two wouldn't need to buy us a wedding present. One had given me my life back and the other had helped me to walk again. Those were pretty incredible gifts. They were, to a great extent, the reason I was there. It was the supreme irony that a few years later I was crying all the way through Maggie's wedding to – believe it or not – a *Mr Walker*.

'Are you OK?' Nick said, when I reached him. 'You look amazing.'

There were lots of tears. Someone played the piano. Darren read the lyrics to a Beatles' song. Lianne and Alex gave a reading. Dad was so proud that when the vicar asked, 'Who gives this woman?' he roared, 'I DO!' at the top of his lungs and the whole congregation clapped thunderously.

Not being tremendous church-going traditionalists, we chose 'If I Had a Hammer' as one of our 'hymns'. I chose it because of that line: 'I'd hammer out love between my brothers and my sisters all over the world'. I hadn't thought about the two previous lines: 'I'd hammer out danger, I'd hammer out a warning'. Maybe it was doubly apt.

In her sermon, Rosie didn't avoid the events of 7/7 either. But she subverted them into something powerful and positive. The words I remember clearly were about 'the love, courage and determination not to be defined by a mindless act of horror'.

When Nick and I were finally pronounced 'man and

wife' everybody cheered. Typical Wright do – even our wedding was noisy.

The reception, at Shendish Manor in Hertfordshire, was sensational. There was a lovely moment during the speeches when my mum stood up and said she'd like to say a word. She'd cried virtually all the way through the wedding but still looked fabulous in her black and white suit, not least because, like me, she'd had her eyelashes dyed. Neither of us could be trusted with mascara on the day.

Her speech was only short but it came right from the heart, addressed to Hasu and Maggie. It was a personal thank you for all they'd done for her daughter. Everyone stood up and cheered.

Everything was going without a hitch. My only worry beforehand was whether I'd manage the steps in and out of the venue on my legs. But they said not to worry; they'd build me a ramp. They were as good as their word. It was a very impressive ramp covered in red carpet and I'd become very well acquainted with it as the party wore on.

After a few hours I wish I'd never asked for it. I had both my wheelchairs on standby, the electric and the manual one, but I stayed on my legs all day and all evening. Better for dancing, and I was so high from excitement and happiness.

I only remember falling down the ramp three times, but I think it happened about six or seven times in total. The first time I went flat on my face you can imagine the uproar: 'Oh, my God, the bride's fallen over! Martine, are you all right?' Everyone in the vicinity rushed to my aid, gently picked me up, brushed me down and fetched me a drink – which might have been part of the problem. I'm told that by the fifth or sixth time the crowd outside smoking just casually looked over and shouted, 'You all right?' Then blithely carried on with their conversation while I rolled around laughing, trying to get up.

I know it's true because our wonderful photographer who captured the whole wedding finished our album with a picture of me lying prone on the carpet.

'I had a feeling you wouldn't mind,' she said, when she presented it to us. 'It seemed to sum up the spirit of the day.' She's right, I don't mind.

Funnily enough, that picture wasn't in *Hello!*

When we booked the Maldives for our honeymoon, I hadn't quite considered that it was one of the most inaccessible destinations in the world. It was my idea of a heavenly holiday, chilling on a beautiful beach by a beautiful sea. It was not, I should add, Nick's idea of the world's greatest trip – a field, as usual, would have suited him better – but he cheered up no end when we were upgraded on the plane.

The service was lovely, including champagne, but it appeared I was something of a rarity. I'd boarded the plane with my legs on but, as this was long haul, I removed them after a while.

'Is there anywhere I can put my legs?' I asked.

They looked at me and the now-detached legs, stunned. But eventually a spot was found for them.

Peace and quiet then broke out in the First Class compartment until about 3 a.m., when the combination of champagne plus lots of water meant that I needed a wee. They went off to fetch me a special aisle chair to wheel me to the on-board toilet.

'Can you get into the chair?' they asked solicitously.

'Oh yeah, fine,' I replied airily, completely missing it and falling on the floor. The stewardess was completely mortified. 'It's fine, it's fine,' I reassured her, rolling around, cracking up.

But clearly they felt they needed to make it up to us for the misfire because a few hours later, as we readied ourselves to leave the plane, they proudly presented us with a cake. Nick had a large thought bubble coming out of his head saying: 'What the hell are we going to do with a cake?' but I managed to thank them for their kindness and it joined the general juggling act of legs, wheelchair and suitcases that our entourage involved.

At least we'd reached the Maldives. What could possibly go wrong? This I found out within moments, as my suitcase was apprehended at the airport scanner for further investigation. I'd completely forgotten what I'd packed but was pretty relaxed there was nothing sharp or dangerous in there.

The security woman rummaged around a little and pulled out a set of pink fluffy handcuffs that I'd been

presented with at my hen night. Oh, my God. I was absolutely mortified.

'Are these yours?' she asked with careful neutrality.

'Yeah, well, er . . .'

'I will have to confiscate them,' she explained.

'Yes, yes, please DO confiscate them, quickly.' The
shame!

'You will need to fill out a form and when you come
back through the airport they will be returned to you.'

'No, no, it's fine. I don't need them back.'

'Here is the form. Where it says "item" you need to
write "handcuffs, pink".'

'No, that's fine, don't worry. We'll manage.'

A large queue had formed behind us, watching the
exchange with interest, and even Nick had noticed what
was going on.

'What the hell?' he said, appalled. 'What did you bring
them for?'

As yet, I thought to myself, this is not quite the honeymoon of my dreams.

However, one small plane and one motorboat later we
were in our villa with its own massive granite pool.
When I mentioned to our butler – butler! – that I couldn't
shower because I had nothing to sit on, he came back
forty minutes later with a beautiful wooden bench that
one of their workmen had just made. It was an incredible
place.

For the last few days we moved to a lovely water

bungalow, not so much by the sea, as in it. The floors were made of glass, so you could see the water underneath. Unfortunately it was a little bit windy and wet by then, which made Nick slightly nervous.

There was a time when I'd have said, 'Oh don't be stupid, it's fine.' It's a bit of a Wright thing that. We can be mistaken for over-confident. It can come across as being a bit dismissive of other people's feelings and it winds Nick up. And after all we'd been through, I controlled my urge to say things along the lines of, 'Pull yourself together. Life's not that bad.'

Instead I tried to cheer him up another way. I suggested we both have a gorgeous treatment to make ourselves feel better. I had a massage with hot stones, which was so wonderful it made me cry. As in sob uncontrollably. It was incredible. I drowned in tears for a while. It was like a long, long-needed release. I thought Nick might have experienced something similar, and caught up with him to find out. He'd chosen a session of Reiki.

'How was yours?' I asked, by now almost deliriously relaxed.

'The most uncomfortable hour I've ever had,' he replied, as he described a lengthy session with a gentle young man massaging his inner thighs. He didn't unclench his muscles for about five hours. So much for relaxation!

* * *

In time, it was natural to think about children. I didn't know if I could have kids, after the whole physical trauma my body had been through. The doctors had no idea either. Nick and I weren't spring chickens. We were in uncharted territory. So, with typical enthusiasm, I decided to help things on a bit. I became a dedicated follower of my ovulation cycles, involving the unromantic business of peeing on sticks.

Poor Nick became used to me calling him at work and instructing him to come home quickly. Or he'd be working in his photographic studio at home when I'd burst in. 'Hurry up. Now!' It's hardly the way to conduct a sensitive love life but . . . it worked.

After a while I had a feeling I might be pregnant, so I visited a branch of Boots in disguise (as if it's easy to disguise yourself in a wheelchair) for the testing kit. I waited with mounting impatience to get it home again, where I locked myself in the grotty bathroom we had at the time and held my breath, waiting for the result. Please, please, please, I silently pleaded. A little blue cross appeared. Amazing.

'Oh, my God, Nick, I'm pregnant,' I announced, as I wheeled myself out of the bathroom. He fell to his knees beside me and we hugged one another. We were probably both thinking two things simultaneously: one, fantastic. Two, holy shit, now what was going to happen?

It gradually became more real as we told people. I especially remember Mum's reaction. I'd managed to find tickets for her and I to see Take That's first reunion the following July, now bang on my due date. She's a massive fan and was really looking forward to it. So it was with a degree of mischief I called her up and said: 'Look, I don't know whether I can go to Take That after all.'

'Oh no,' she said. I could hear the utter disappointment in her voice.

'Yeah . . . *because I'm pregnant!*' Cue screams and tears.

I remember Tanni Grey-Thompson, one of Britain's greatest ever female Paralympians, saying that when she was pregnant a complete stranger came up while she was just wheeling along the street and said, 'My God, how did that happen?' Well, clearly she and I are examples of people who follow the rules of biology. Being human.

When I told my GP the good news she produced one of those little wheely dial gadgets that work out when your due date will be.

'Hmm,' she said, twirling it around. 'Yes, this says you'll be due on . . . the 7 July.'

What?' I screamed.

'What?' she cried back, wondering what the hell was the matter.

'7 of July. 7/7!' I prompted.

'Oh God,' she said. 'Well, you know these things aren't always accurate. It's just a guide. Babies are rarely on time.' She turned out to be right there.

At the beginning of the pregnancy, things went pretty well. I didn't get morning sickness particularly, I managed to say on my legs for the first four months, and I developed a commendable passion for ginger and elderflower cordial, which I drank by the gallon. I also had cravings for satsumas (healthy) and crumpets (not). So much so that Nick started calling the bump 'Crumpet', as though I was breeding a giant bun.

It was hard at times though. Pregnancy was obviously a big, big, big thing for me. I was tired, my balance was disrupted, and I was often scared I was going to fall over. After the fourth month, having to be in my wheelchair all the time was not good for me psychologically. I thought I looked a bit weird. It sapped my confidence. I'd always felt more comfortable around people if I was able to wear my legs.

But, never mind. Nick and I went to the local National Childbirth Trust group, as you do as first-time parents, and we properly absorbed all the information: 'You may want to take candles into the birthing room.' Oh yeah, I thought, must buy candles. Tick that box. 'Your husband might want to make up a selection of your favourite music.' Yes, Nick. Including the now-banished Take That. Obviously my birth plan would involve no drugs. No, no, no, never. Did I want to have the baby in a birthing pool? Did I? Nick and I looked at each other in wonder. Sounded good. I told the consultant.

There was a big hoo-ha about it. The consultant was concerned about me having a baby in the first place. Her big fear was that if a medical emergency happened, would

I be able to get out of the pool? The midwife said yes, it wouldn't be a problem. She'd just haul me out if necessary. But there seemed to be a big question mark hanging over the whole thing.

So the due date arrived – 7 July – and nothing happened. Nothing at all. And so it went on for another fifteen days, during which I ate more and more jalfrezi curries to hurry things along, with no effect but to make me ever more massive. I tried raspberry leaf tea with pineapple. Nothing.

In the end I went into hospital, baby unbudged, because there was a bit of a scare over an irregular heartbeat. That proved to be a false alarm but, as I was there, they decided the time had come to induce me. I took the pill and nothing happened. The word 'caesarean' started to be aired. I really didn't want that. I was very scared about what that would mean for me. It would have a devastating effect on my movement. How would I get out of my chair? I'd convinced myself that natural childbirth was the way to go, and I just couldn't let a caesarean happen.

But by the third day in hospital, and a third pill with no result, I was bawling my eyes out. I was in a maternity ward with women disappearing at frequent intervals and then coming back with little bundles in their arms while I was still sitting there, mammothly uncomfortable and desperate. Luckily I suddenly spotted my consultant over the other side of the ward. I dispatched Nick, ever hovering, to fetch her.

'Look,' I said, 'I feel ill. I'm not ill. I'm pregnant. Why can't we sort this out?'

She did. About an hour later I was moved to a room. A surgeon arrived, I was hooked to a machine and, immediately, a really, really intense pain began. There was no question of getting used to it by slow build-up. It was there and terrible. Poor Nick. It's got to be the worst experience anyone can go through to witness someone you love suffering that kind of pain.

'Do you want your music?' he asked desperately. I screamed. The whole natural childbirth thing went out the window.

After eighteen hours of this, he went out and came back again with fish and chips. 'Do you want a chip?' he asked tentatively. When I yelled, 'Get away from me!' at top volume he worked out that I didn't. The midwife could see how stressed he was and suggested he go for a coffee. I didn't even notice at the time, being by now full of drugs but still resisting an epidural with all my might.

I can't quite remember how 'No, no, no, not an epidural' became 'Yes, yes, yes, I want an epidural and I want it NOW', but it did.

'OK,' they said. 'It should be along in a couple of hours.'

A COUPLE OF HOURS! They might as well have said a billion years. Then they told me I was just five centimetres dilated. Jesus. Not more than halfway there. That's when the medical profession and I decided a caesarean was probably the way to go.

Only a couple of hours before the caesarean I had the epidural. One minute I was screaming like a banshee, the next I was sitting up in bed turning the pages of a magazine. When the time came for the operation, they put up a screen so that Nick (at the head end) and I couldn't see what was going on. The only part I found daunting was lying back with a mask on my face. I had a sort of panic attack and thought I couldn't breathe, probably because it took me back to my previous time in hospital, in the intensive care unit.

But then we heard the words 'What a big baby!' and everything but relief and joy faded away. They pulled down the screen and there he was – a baby boy. I could hear them having a sweepstake on how heavy he was, because he was so massive. He was ten pounds, and I'm no more than a metre tall. No wonder he didn't want to come out. I reckon he must have grown a good deal while I was eating all those jalfrezis.

We took him back to the maternity ward and I stayed in for another four days while 'Oscar', as we had now named him, recovered from jaundice in one of those special little cots. The whole place rang to the sound of crying, and probably not just the babies. All of us mums were sitting there, shell-shocked and thinking, What the hell . . . ?

But the time had come to go home; that moment new parents both long for and dread. *Here's the baby, you're on your own.* Oscar, naturally, wouldn't stop crying on his first night. We were at Mum's because the builders were in our place up the road, so there was I, probably not the first or last new mum on the phone to the hospital, semi-sobbing myself, saying, 'There's something wrong with him.' But of course, he was fine.

I had learned something profound. Being a cool auntie to a baby is not the same as owning one. I had a feeling this would be quite an adventure. Looking back, we made mistakes, but you learn quickly. If I could go back and offer myself some advice for those early days of babyhood I'd probably say, number one, relax.

Other hints:

- Curries do not bring on labour. All they do is make the baby bigger.
- Thick breast pads are necessary. I shall never forget being at a baby massage class in Tring with about a dozen other mothers I didn't know terribly well, when Oscar decided it was feeding time. As I undid my bra to serve lunch, my milk shot across the room at high velocity, narrowly missing the crowd. Impressive but not especially welcome.
- Never think it's safe to leave a nappy off. Even for a minute.
- You will be exhausted. Get used to it.
- With every little smile, all the tiredness melts away.

7

'The Floor Cleaners'

B elieve me, I didn't set out to become a Paralympian. There were still a few telling differences between me and a superwoman. So it was just for fun that I attended the Amputee Games at Stoke Mandeville Hospital in 2008, encouraged as always by the wonderful Maggie. It was only about five miles up the road from where we were living at the time, so I thought I might as well give it a casual look. She said she'd be there too. Fine. Any excuse to socialise.

I wasn't expecting it to change my life and that afternoon, as I was twanging archery bows and waving fencing swords about, I had absolutely no idea where this comical introduction to disability sport would lead.

I had a go at most things on offer there and clearly I was ticking a few boxes for the organisers. Disabled? Yes. Fit?

Yes-ish. Interested in sport? Yes. If you fell into one of those three categories they were ecstatic. If you ticked all three they were so enthusiastic they wouldn't leave you alone.

'Oh look, you've scored a bull's-eye,' said the archery cheerleader. 'That's absolutely brilliant. Can I have your name and phone number so we can get you to some sessions?' But I didn't really take to it.

'That's terrific stuff,' said the fencing buff, of my Errol Flynn performance with the sword. I stopped them there. I didn't like fencing. I couldn't get used to just sitting back in my wheelchair playing nicely. All I wanted to do was lean forward, brandishing my cutlass, and go for the jugular. Apparently you're not allowed to do that.

'You've definitely got an eye for this,' said the table tennis coordinator, but again I found that being in the wheelchair was constricting and foiled my aggressive instincts with the bat. It was the most frustrating thing. I crossed that one off the list too.

Now, wheelchair tennis – that was more like it. It was difficult to move and hit the ball at the same time but I loved the sense of freedom and space – and whacking the ball as hard as I could. I could get into this, I thought.

And then someone suggested sitting volleyball, which I'd never heard of. It was being demonstrated by a former coach to the Dutch men's team – a high-above-the-knee amputee and lovely man. He showed us how you abandoned your wheelchair to play it. You sat on the floor instead, sliding about on your bum, bashing balls over the net. It looked dynamic, fast-paced and fun. When my turn came, I discovered the on button to my innate sporting competitiveness. I wasn't quite shoving small children out of the way to get to a ball, but pretty nearly. I realised immediately – I love this sport.

All the sports involved were recruiting for the London Paralympics four years later. This was beyond my wildest dreams obviously and even if I was capable of harbouring wild dreams I was told that sitting volleyball had no GB women's team. So that was the end of that. I gravitated towards wheelchair tennis instead, dividing my time between their two training venues in Roehampton and Ruislip. For fun I joined a sitting volleyball club, too, the London Lynx, based at a school on Commercial Road, coincidentally right behind The Royal London Hospital.

I was busy flying about between the two sports, loving the buzz, the challenge, the sheer physicality of them, when I discovered I was pregnant with Oscar. Is it a good idea to throw myself about the volleyball court? I asked myself and answered: No. So I had to give up the Lynx and concentrate on tennis instead, until Oscar's presence became sufficiently felt to give up sport altogether for the time being. That could have been the end of my sports career.

It was October 2009 when I received a call out of nowhere. I was three months into motherhood, shattered and living with Mum while our new house up the road

163

was being converted to take wheelchairs, pushchairs and about a million plastic baby toys. Our whole life was in Mum's spare bedroom including us, big baby, king-size bed, Oscar's Moses basket, my prosthetic legs . . . and into this crazy world comes an invitation to Tottenham Hotspur's ground to try out for the first-ever GB women's sitting volleyball team. Any sane woman in my position would say have said no.

'Yes,' I said.

I had no idea how many people would turn up. There might be hundreds. I stood no chance. In fact, there were five of us there, and two of those were blokes. I immediately liked the two other women involved: Claire Harvey, a former Scottish rugby player, prison governor and mother of two children, who had suffered a spinal cord injury in an accident, and Helen Sole, a school teacher, a mum and a double amputee, having been born with a congenital leg condition. 'Which was quite a shock for my poor old mum,' she said.

We bonded pretty well on the day but what were the chances of us reconvening as the hardcore of a Paralympic sitting volleyball team? I'd have said somewhere around nil. A few days later, I heard from the organisers again – I was in. I was, temporarily anyway, in the squad trying out for the London Paralympics. It seemed ridiculous. Nick had no idea what was going on. To him it was just a sport I was doing in my spare time between the odd bit of work and being Oscar's mum. But in my mind I was already crossing into new and significant territory.

Sitting volleyball was a sport developed after the Second World War as something that injured soldiers could play to help with their mental and physical recovery. It had become popular all over Europe as a sport for the disabled except, for some reason, in the UK. I've no idea why that was. It's the only Paralympic sport that allows you to play sitting down but not in a wheelchair.

I loved the physicality and camaraderie of it. The sense of freedom when we all abandoned our wheelchairs or chucked prosthetic legs out of the way was intoxicating. Legs were a positive nuisance; they got in the way. For the first time in my life my new physical format turned out to be a significant advantage. Some people nicknamed us 'The Floor Cleaners' for the obvious reason that we polished up the courts we played on to a gleaming shine with our bums. I bet the real cleaners at these places loved us.

More players were being attracted by British Volleyball to join us. Emma Wiggs arrived, a PE teacher with real drive and determination, whose legs had been paralysed by a random virus she'd picked up during her gap year working on a sheep farm in Australia. I immediately warmed to her on the grounds that she came from Watford. We were practically geographical sisters. And when I found out her old PE teacher was the wife of my friend Alex's sister-in-law, I thought the coincidences were getting spooky. Some people might say that's stretching it! But I really, really believed these chance connections were trying to tell me something.

My double life as sportswoman/mum was exhausting. After five or six hours of jumping around on a court at weekends in training, I couldn't believe how knackered I was. We'd go away to glamorous places like Kettering, where the junior volleyball team was based, to train and stay overnight in single beds designed for students rather than mums in their thirties. It wasn't that we were junior; we just had no money and this was the best compromise.

If – and at this stage it was a huge IF – our coach could whip us into shape in time, we were still on course for that Paralympic spot, but there were mountainous hurdles to overcome. First would be the World Championships in Oklahoma in the summer of 2010. I'd warmed up for this event by winning my first cap at a tournament in Kent, to which the Paralympic champions, China, had been invited as our opposition. This was a bit like pushing me on court with a tennis racquet and saying, go on then, have a go against Serena Williams. Well, Serena Williams sitting down, I suppose.

We feared the worst but then had our hopes raised by the sight of the entire Chinese team scoffing McDonald's just before the start of the match. Maybe we'd defeat them thanks to their accute indigestion. They were made of sterner stuff. We were annihilated. Nick and Oscar had come to watch me. I don't think either of them was particularly impressed, and my son slept through most of it in a papoose.

The best part of the Kent trip involved Claire's dark sense of humour, when she went to complain that the accommodation we were staying in was infested with ants. She was dismissed by a completely bored and unresponsive member of the management, so she came back to fetch me. This time we both turned up, with me legless, as it were, in my wheelchair.

'You don't understand the seriousness of this,' said Claire, pointing to me. 'She had legs last night when she went to bed . . .'

I can't remember whether we got upgraded from our ants' nest but it was worth the effort just to see this woman's face.

I was terribly torn about going to Oklahoma. I knew I had to go to stand any chance of getting into the Paralympics, but I'd miss Oscar's first birthday. I'd be away for two-and-a-half weeks, which was a hell of a long time. I took soundings from friends and family. 'Look, don't worry. He's only one. He won't even remember.' I sort of knew they were right but I still felt deeply guilty. I Skyped him from the States during his birthday party, but he was far more interested in his cheese sandwich than talking to his mum.

We'd flown to America, I could scarcely believe it, on 7 July – another one for my coincidence collection. 'You couldn't make this up,' I'd say to any of the team who came within range on the flight. They were getting used to me and my ever-growing feelings of destiny. Not that it always brought me good luck. Upon disembarking after the transatlantic flight, I discovered that my one wheelchair had been seriously damaged in the hold. It now had a jerk and a wobble when it moved. The girls found this indescribably funny: a disabled athlete complete with disabled wheelchair.

It was no way to begin a global event that could decide our future, up against the greatest and, in many cases, fully professional teams in the world. We were little more than enthusiastic amateurs at this stage. Apart from Emma, who was now captain, and Claire, few of us were born-and-bred athletes. We'd been drawn into this new existence by accident and disability. We were quite a crowd: Andrea, a physio from Derby, a bit older than me, whose back condition, which caused a drop foot, hadn't stopped her playing standing volleyball in the past; tall Jess from Wales with a club foot; Jay, a bit of a teenage wild child, and Amy, a girl in her early twenties, who reminded me of me when I was her age, up for a beer and a social. Then there was Olga, from Latvia – a double amputee with, we noticed after a while, no thumbs but five fingers on each hand. She was permanently baffled by the British sense of humour, spending most of her time frowning while asking, 'What are you laughing about now?' And when we told her, she'd reply, 'That's not funny.' Which, in itself, was very funny.

We did our best in Oklahoma but found the task

monumentally tough. Just propelling a wheelchair in fifty-degree heat from the accommodation block to the sports hall – about 100 metres – was enough to drench you in sweat, never mind the actual play. It was our first real taste of what we might expect if we reached the Paralympics. We got battered. But I do remember making a couple of really good blocks against the Chinese No.12, one of the best players in the world, who looked about seven feet tall to me. She had a massive hit on her and one of these missiles was coming straight for me at the net. I shut my eyes, put my hand up to protect myself and we won the point with a brilliant instinctive block. OK, it was somewhat fortunate, but I'd already discovered in life that you have to make your own luck.

I'm pretty sure we ran the Japanese quite close in one of our matches too, but my memories tend to wander towards the random moments surrounding the competition rather than the shots, blocks and disappointing results. For a start we had to choose the shirt numbers on our new national kit. I wanted number seven. Of course, everybody wanted number seven, for various reasons. It was someone's lucky number. It was someone's birthday. It was their dog's birthday. It was Ronaldo's shirt number and they loved him.

'I want number seven,' I said, 'because I got blown up that day.'

There was a terrible silence followed by everyone shouting at once.

'Oh, God, take it. Take it. TAKE IT!' I took it with a big grin. Shameless.

We were not downcast by the results. We knew it would be difficult, and it was, but we had learned so much we actually felt pleased. It was time for a little celebration at the closing ceremony, which included free tickets to the local theme park. It had been years since I'd been on a rollercoaster and never once since I'd lost my legs. But it looked safe enough; a funny, rickety, wooden affair that swooshed up and down through the trees. I went on with Claire, which was a good thing, as she probably saved me from flying out of the carriage. I had no idea how hard it would be to keep myself locked in without the ballast of legs. We could both feel me lifting off the seat and she had to clutch me for dear life while I helpfully screamed.

As a result we needed a beer. This meant a walk/wheel to the 7-Eleven store, which caused terrible confusion for our brilliant assistant coach and packhorse, Karen.

'It's 9 p.m. though,' she said. 'It might be shut.'

'It's the 7-ELEVEN!' we chorused.

'Yeah, but it's late. It's probably closed.'

'It's the 7-ELEVEN!' we yelled, to be explicit.

'I know, but I don't think it will be open this late.'

And so on. She's a senior executive in JP Morgan now.

Looking back, I can't imagine a more wide-ranging team of individuals. Most teams at least have their moulding as a teenage athlete in common, even if they're different shapes and sizes. But us – we were different ages, from teenage to over forty; we had different backgrounds, including mums, teachers, café owners, students and a former prison governor; there were different levels of disability, some minimal, some profound, and different nationalities in Welsh Jess and Latvian Olga. There were different expectations, different sexualities – from straight to bisexual to gay – and different degrees of commitment, especially among the youngsters like Amy, Jay and Chloe, who had only very recently lost a leg below the knee.

Andrea, Jess and a talented player called Lou were our 'Minimally Disabled' players. They were a very important part of the set-up because the rules of sitting volleyball allow one 'MD' on the court at any one time alongside the five disabled players. All players have to be classified as one or the other, and it's one of the very few areas in life where you want to be seen as disabled as possible. There was some kind of clerical error at the Euros in Holland in 2011 when I was pulled aside for reclassification. This astounded me. You've either got two legs or you haven't. There isn't much room for doubt. 'They haven't grown back. I'm not sitting on them. They're not here,' I said, helpfully, during the process.

Sometimes, though, the reclassification process wasn't so funny. Lou was devastated to be told before London that her knee injury was no longer severe enough to warrant classification as an MD. They said it might become so again later. That was scant consolation to someone now barred from competing at their home Paralympics. We were all distraught. She was one of our best players. It exemplified the fiendishly fine line between a Paralympic-approved disability and having a bad knee. If you crossed some notional border by a millimetre, that was it. Out.

The degree of coming and going in the team was quite challenging. We were often in a state of flux, and even within the people sticking around there were obvious points of contention. While Claire and Emma didn't particularly get on, I was good friends with both of them. I thought Claire was ridiculously accomplished, balancing sport with family and a high-powered job at the Financial Services Authority in London. She had a wicked sense of humour, as witnessed in the 'ants' incident. Emma was sparky, funny and formidably driven.

It was the first time I'd been around gay women in my life, although I knew loads of gay men in my clubbing days. I noticed for about a minute and then didn't. These girls were characters, teammates, laughs, shoulders to cry on. The categories – and my God we covered most of them – made no difference at all.

Vicky joined us soon after the World Championships – an easy-going, northern future psychoanalyst with ginger hair (which we obviously hailed as her disability) who had been brought in as another MD. Bizarrely she's one of the very few people in Britain who were alive at the time, but who have no memory of 7/7 at all. She'd come off her motorbike and was in a coma when it happened. There's a coincidence – both of us were in hospital for different reasons at the same time.

From a very early stage we, as a team, had to learn about each other. We all had to know what made the others tick and where particular sensitivities lay. We also, crucially, had to know the limits of our physical capabilities. On court we were utterly dependent on one another; our reach, our smash, our powers of movement, were key to this dynamic game. Minus legs, I had the advantage of moving incredibly fast, which earned me the nickname 'Flying Monkey', taken from *The Wizard of Oz* and the 'Mexican Jumping Bean'. Not especially politically correct, but we traded in non-PC jokes all the time. The worse the better.

Emma and I used have a go at each other on court for laughs.

'You've got no legs,' she'd taunt me if I missed a shot.

'Well, you've got legs and they're bloody useless,' I'd say.

One year, she bought me socks for Christmas. I thrived on the jokes. It was a safe place to be appallingly rude to one another. The relief was tremendous because, in another part of my life, a serious event was playing out at the same time.

Not long after our return from America I'd been summoned to give evidence at the inquest into the 7/7 bombings. I was prepared for the memories this would stir up, but less so the disturbing revelations – to my mind, at least – in the media. Nick and the rest of the family tried to hide newspapers from me if they thought something might upset me but it was impossible. I'd find myself studying diagrams of the Aldgate carriage with its little stick men and women in the positions they had occupied when the bomb was detonated. They were in different colours: green for the women, black for the men. Red for the dead. To see it laid out so clinically like that upset me very much.

Nick came with me on the day and I met Liz Kenworthy, the policewoman who had first reached me in the train carriage, briefly in the waiting room before giving evidence. She was coming out as I was going in. I'd heard her talking on the live video link in the room beforehand, when she explained that my legs had been damaged beyond help in the explosion. My left leg in particular had been fused to the side of the carriage in the force and heat of the blast. They'd virtually melted into one another. A long time ago I'd wondered if my legs, or at least one of them, could have been saved. Now I knew why they couldn't.

The coroner, Lady Justice Hallett, was very kind in taking evidence. I told her about my strong memory of Liz coming through the train door and how she had given me a belt to tie round my right leg to stop me bleeding to death. 'I knew in my head she saved my life,' I said. But I also talked about getting married, having Oscar, who was fourteen months old by now, and the continuing dream of representing my country as a Paralympian.

When I stepped down the coroner said, 'Your story is truly inspirational – the triumph of human spirit over dreadful adversity.' She wished me luck in my Paralympic quest.

That is what it had become: a quest, a mission to achieve the nearly impossible. We were a 'band of sisters'. That was the slightly cheesy name given to us by documentary makers for Channel 4 in the build-up to London 2012. A film crew was going to follow us for a few weeks, covering training sessions and a competition in Finland. This was big-time stuff. Other films in the series included Dave Clarke, the captain of the GB visually impaired football team and Lee Pearson, the multi Paralympic gold-winning dressage rider. Both of them wonderful, motivational, influential figures.

Our episode opened with me pushing a wheelchair down a hill in the snow towards a lake saying, 'Going down's fine actually,' and immediately falling over backwards, where I lay waving my arms to make angel wings in a snow drift. That pretty much set the tone. It was definitely more comedy than drama.

The commentary described our Paralympic ambition as 'an audacious dream', which was quite tactful of them in the circumstances. Action switched to the Roehampton gym, where a number of us were sitting on the floor trying to heave ourselves up a rope. The camera zooms in on red faces and straining noises, but no one's bum actually leaves the ground.

'With a professional training team and dedicated facilities, there are hopes of creating a high-performance team with medals to follow,' the commentary went on, with model optimism.

Imogen, one of our most recent recruits, confided a sporting tip to the camera: 'One way of keeping your eye make-up on while sweating profusely is to squirt hair spray over it.' She then bravely revealed the team's cigarette collection and admitted her sporting development had a way to go. 'Obviously I'm still poo at the moment,' she said.

A British Paralympic Association assessor arrived to monitor our progress. She explained that we would be watched closely over a six-month period, and if we hadn't made the necessary improvements we would not qualify for the Games.

'It'll mean sacrifices – eating, drinking, the whole lot,' she was telling Emma Wiggs, who nodded in agreement. Our new coach, Steve, took up the refrain, asking us to think about certain things.

'Do I need that extra doughnut? Do I need that extra cigarette?'

I wasn't sure the *extra* ones were the issue.

Pressure had been piled onto the Finland tournament. We knew that poor performances would shatter our London hopes, but first we had to negotiate the culture shock. The people were very friendly but they bewildered us at first by offering us the chance to get into their 'ass-hole'.

'Pardon?' we said, unsure of the context.

'Yes, do you want to get into the *ass-hole* ... a famous thing to do in Finland?'

'Er ... no,' we said, politely. 'No, we'd prefer not to do that.'

'Yes,' they said, pointing to a hole in the snow. 'Very good for the heart.'

'Oh, OH, yes, I see. The *ice hole*, not the, er ... yes, thank you.'

That was a relief.

Of course we had to go in. I still possess a bunch of photos for blackmail purposes of a group of us standing around in the snow in swimming cossies – even some lunatics in bikinis (not me) – before plunging into black water, too shocked by the cold to scream. I managed three short breaststrokes before thinking I was going to die. The pain was like sharks biting you and the clambering out was not ladylike. It was a panicky launch up a set of rough steps made of ice, and it scraped your bum like a scourer.

'Ah, yes, very good for you,' we said to our hosts later, with tinges of sarcasm, after three hours in the sauna to thaw out.

The whole setup was new to us, and one or two facets caught us by surprise. Like the time Claire and I were wandering down a narrow corridor after a sauna, only to see two butt-naked guys from the male Slovakian goalball team heading away from us. They each had a towel about the size of a flannel. They were obviously 'looking' for the sauna, as far as guys who are visually impaired can look. Instead they were about to open the outside door and step starkers into the snow. Claire and I watched, horribly fascinated, wondering whether we should shout a warning. The potential for embarrassment or frostbite was massive. Luckily they somehow divined their error and corrected themselves, which meant walking back up the corridor and squeezing past us.

'My God,' Claire whispered (let's hope quietly enough not to be heard), 'that's the first full-sized willy I've ever seen.'

International incidents aside, these continental tournaments were crucial to us. It was all very well training but we needed to be battle-hardened. On the other hand we were cash-starved, so we couldn't go to all the tournaments our competitors were playing. Some of us used to pay our own way occasionally if we considered an event to be vital. It meant we took smaller squads abroad than we would have liked, and we certainly stayed in some dodgy places.

One of the worst was a gruesome building in Hungary, which we discovered had been a former mental institution. To see its décor was like stepping back thirty years. The shower facilities were just an overhead tap above a concrete floor. Emma and I found an old wooden bench, which we somehow dragged into the toilets, and then got someone to turn a hose on us. Cold water. This was not far short of torture. It was at this point I realised how huge my commitment had become to the goal of becoming a Paralympian.

Claire's response to the no-go shower conundrum was typically no-nonsense. She just sat on the concrete floor and turned the tap on. There were no niceties like shower curtains, so when one of men's team walked in to take a shower he was confronted with a naked Claire on the floor and she was confronted with – well, her eye-line was at groin level.

'Wosser's bits were dangling right in front of my face,' as she put it later.

They both screamed. He beat a retreat and the rest of us laughed for days. One way or another, Claire's experiences were developing quite a theme.

There were two final competitions in 2011/2012 that, for us, were make or break. The first was the Intercontinental Cup in Ukraine, one of the biggest tournaments in the sitting volleyball calendar. We knew how vital this was. And then we all went down with food poisoning. The meals were indescribable, featuring powdered egg and tongue. Tongue of what, they didn't say. Vicky was vegetarian, which meant cucumber and some sort of terrible gnocchi substance for breakfast, lunch and dinner. When she asked for dessert she was given the same gnocchi, now sprinkled with sugar.

I shared a room with Emma, Claire and an abundance

of flies, and even though we tried everything to get rid of them, there was one that never seemed to go. In the end we named it 'Mooha', Russian for 'fly', and treated it like a mascot.

At least we had our kettle. Wherever we went the first thing we did was rummage for the kettle and put on a cup of tea. We brought enough biscuits and tea bags to open a corner shop. As time went by we adjusted the merchandise from fig rolls and chocolate biscuits to malt loaf and flapjacks, on the tenuous grounds they were healthier.

The competition ranked as progress. Fuelled by flapjacks we did OK, but it was the post-competition party that proved particularly interesting. We were up for a dance but not nearly as much as one of the MDs on the Ukrainian team. We'd understood she couldn't bend her knees due to some unfortunate condition, but come a burst of samba music and she was bumping and grinding all over the floor. We obviously filmed and photographed the event for the authorities but nothing ever happened as far as I know.

I wonder now whether we were one of the last sports teams allowed into that particular area. We were in the Crimea, right on the Black Sea, now close to a notorious war zone. Yet I remember it fondly as the place Olga used to rush down to the beach with her towel and suntan lotion and where, for some crazy reason, we bought Karen a blow-up rubber ring in the shape of a frog.

No one could doubt our spirit. But had we done enough

to convince the BPA we were good enough for London? Our last chance to shine was in Egypt where, such were the security concerns, we had our own personal body-guard. He used to get on the coach with us between our accommodation and Cairo's sports area; two guns visible in their holsters. We could tell our hotel was close to some military establishment because we'd be woken early in the morning by the sound of marching boots. The hotel itself seemed to have enjoyed a lurid history. Our corridor was memorable for the imprint of a bloodied hand on the wall.

Had we done enough training to deserve our place? God, it felt like it. By 2012 the doughnuts had gone and it was protein, protein, protein. Boiled eggs were every-where. Whenever I left the house my mind automatically chanted: 'Phone, keys, boiled egg.' I'd frequently open my training bag and find a random egg that had been in there two weeks.

Kettering was in the past. We moved on to a special training base at Roehampton University; facilities we shared with other sports and the PE students on campus. This brought on another of my famous coincidences. As I stood outside our training centre I could see the window of my old room at the Douglas Bader Unit. The room that used to be smothered in get-well cards sent in by members of the public. They'd worked, those cards. I had got well.

Even so, my stamina was being truly tested. The sched-ule was punishing. We couldn't afford full-time training so we condensed thirty-five hours into three days, from Saturday mornings to Tuesday mornings, when we tottered back to our lives, exhausted. Monday was the killer, a 5 a.m. to 10.30 p.m. marathon, after which we rushed back to our rented house on campus for poached egg and beans at midnight, knowing we had to get up at 5 a.m. again on Tuesday morning for one last session of training.

Shaving minutes, even seconds, off everything we did became important when we were so stretched for time. I'd perfected the art of slinging my wheelchair uncollapsed into the boot of my Vauxhall Zafira for the short journey from the house to our training centre. I would go in with it and then jump into the driving seat. All I needed was one of the girls to be on hand to open the boot and let me out again.

On one memorable occasion they all rushed off, forgetting me, leaving me stuck in my car in the pouring rain, knocking on the windows at oblivious passers-by. Eventually I attracted the attention of some poor unsuspecting teenage boy, probably in his freshers' week, whose first shock was seeing me yell at him out of the window. His second shock was opening the boot to find a woman with no legs sitting in the back of her car, vaguely hysterical and about to kill her teammates.

Mishaps apart, the house was a blessing, a vast improvement on the previous arrangement, which had been to squeeze into a student flat shared by Emma, Vicky, Sam,

Amy and Jay, the teenage wild child who would disappear to have a baby before she came back to the squad in time for London 2012. These living conditions were not ideal. Kipping on a blow-up mattress on Emma's floor for a few hours each night was hardly the recipe for a perfect weekend's training.

We moaned. There was proper unrest in the camp for a while. We had reached the point where we knew we needed to train more, both individually and definitely as a team. But there was next-to-no money to support us. It didn't help that for some bizarre reason British Volleyball were very keen on investing part of their funding in hundreds of volleyball badges, which we were supposed to give out to other teams and supporters. The amount of bloody badges we gave out was ridiculous, and we didn't get any presents back. I thought it was a waste of time.

There were teams we played twelve times, and we'd give a badge to them every time. They had little smirks on their faces, as if to say: 'You're not going to give me a badge are you?' Oh yes, I am, I'd think grimly. It reached the point where we all point-blank refused to give out any more from sheer mortification.

The tensions were becoming evident. Emma, the thorough professional, was a stark contrast to some of the youngsters, both boys and girls, who regarded a Saturday night after training in London as the opportunity to go out and get rat-arsed, smoke fags and have a kebab on the way home.

There were two distinct camps forming and, between them, we were trying to bridge a huge gap between ages, characters, passions and commitment. In the 'oldies' camp there was me, Claire, Andrea, Helen, Emma and Karen. Vicky made guest star appearances in that group but preferred to float; not unlike Jodi, a café owner from Southampton whose leg was amputated after falling off a balcony.

She'd found us, or rather we found her, via Maggie, because she had also done her rehabilitation at Roehampton. She was honest, chatty and astute and wouldn't suffer fools. She was also an insomniac, which meant that if you shared a room with her it was like trying to wake a teenager the next morning.

Sam had joined us by now too – a Welsh former boxer who had served in the British Army in Iraq and was still suffering the effects of PTSD. She'd been the victim of a mortar attack on her army base in a nighttime raid and had received a permanent injury to her right leg from flying shrapnel.

And then there were the 'young 'uns': Jay, Amy and Jess. Many of us were literally old enough to be their mothers, yet somehow we had to gel as a team, as well as persuade them to stop eating kebabs and getting pissed. Julie was a young 'un, too, just thirteen, so she stayed at home with her family. For some reason I felt it was my role to act as the unofficial liaison between both camps, but you could definitely feel the pressure building. The atmosphere

Me on bench. Come on, GB!

London 2012. GB vs Japan.

Waving to the crowd in absolute amazement.

My favourite picture from London 2012. First Paralympic game and fighting back the tears when I saw my family in the crowd.

Five in a bed and the little one said . . .

Douglas Bader Queen Mary's dream team and teammate Jodi.

GB vs the Netherlands. Number one fans Oscar and nephew Felix.

Captain (Claire) and vice-captain (me) celebrating fiftieth cap at London 2012.

The team with Barbara Windsor and Boris Johnson, 2012.

GB men and women the morning after the closing ceremony, feeling a little jaded.

Heroes' parade, London – Vicky and I waving to the unbelievable crowds lining the streets to support us.

Trafalgar Square.

Cathy Stoker, artist, at Pride Art Exhibition, London 2012.

First public speaking experience – TEDx Talk, London 2012.

Huge honour receiving the Helen Rollason Award at SPOTY 2012.

My guardian angel – Liz Kenworthy with family at SPOTY after presenting me with the award.

Claire and me with our new mate, Martina Navratilova.

10 Downing Street, International Women's Day.

Well and truly Strictlyfied for Sport Relief 2014.

Emotional day – Tenth anniversary of 7/7 at St Paul's Cathedral – my family with the famous cockney Bow bells of St Mary-le-Bow church in the distance.

On our way to Wimbledon 2015 – my first time on the tube since 7/7.

At Wimbledon, having a celebratory drink.

Star struck – meeting Colin Firth and wife Liv, fellow judges for the *Observer* Ethical Awards.

The gorgeous Jo Brand, Sport Relief 2016. We laughed a lot!

My first appearance on the BBC as a commentator – Invictus Games 2014.

Invictus Games, Walt Disney, Florida, 2016.

With fellow commentator Chris Mitchell.

Channel 4 Rio Paralympics presenting team.

I've made it – Rio Paralympics 2016.

Me and the lovely Clare Balding.

Returning from Rio. Finally I get my gold medal!

Collecting my MBE from the Princess Royal at the Palace. One of the proudest days of my life.

Outside the Palace with the family.

More MBE celebrations – Mum, Alicia, Matilda, Tracey, Grant and me.

Big balloons, big surprise MBE party, great friends.

Family day out – Oscar, Nick, me, Jim, our family liaison officer (behind me), Tracey, Tyler, Mum, Maureen and Dad.

Fun times with our adopted Mosley family.

On holiday – Tara, Jo, Claire, Shirley, Kelly, Michelle and me.

Me, Nick and Oscar – happy days!

between us all was becoming ever more emotionally charged.

Something had to give. Steve decided to swap Claire into the captaincy role, maybe because her combined experience as a mum and prison governor could be useful in the circumstances. She was probably a bit more commercially savvy, too, after spending years in the business world. It was tough on Emma, and I really felt for her, but it would all come right in the end for her one day in Rio in 2016. I'd be there to witness it, but that story would unfold later.

Right now, personally, I was in a state. As more and more demands were made on us I became powerfully torn in two different directions. I was driving 130 miles a day sometimes to Roehampton and back and I worked out I spent £3,000 a year on petrol. I was shattered and sick with the amount of relentless physical work we were doing. Oscar was still very young and I often had to get up with him in the night when I was home. I was irritable with Nick, who was trying to balance his wedding photography business with childcare. On top of that I felt guilty about leaving Oscar for such long periods. It was a tremendously emotional time.

I missed him taking his first steps. I missed him saying his first words. I missed his first birthday. I was constantly thinking, What the hell am I doing? I'd leave home sometimes slamming the door in Nick's face after a ruck to the sound of Oscar wailing. I'd arrive at training bleary-eyed – partly from lack of sleep and partly from sobbing all the way round the M25 out of sheer guilt. I'd convinced myself that Oscar was suffering terrible separation anxiety and would be in therapy by the time he was eighteen.

Is it worth it? I'd ask myself. But somewhere deep down I had this belief that if I could just keep going then good things would come of it. What Nick found hard was the lack of guarantees. After all this gut-busting effort, the GB women's sitting volleyball team still might not be good enough to make the Games. Even if it did, I might not personally be part of it. We were a group of particularly strong, independent women but the pressure was immense.

At least we could feel ourselves stealthily getting fitter. Our bums were sore, our arms ached, but our weight was going down, our muscle mass going up. That was gratifying. We were constantly measured and assessed. One medical form required our respective heights. I knew I was five foot three inches in my prosthetic legs but the girls insisted that wasn't good enough. The 'without legs' length was necessary too.

They insisted I lay down on the coffee table and measured me with a school ruler. I came to 98 centimetres. We all thought it was a huge joke. If you had any sensitivity at the start of your Paralympic career, you rarely did after a few weeks with a team. Political correctness didn't come into it. We took the mickey out of ourselves, each other and everything else. It was probably the most bonding thing we did – in the obvious absence of pub nights.

I thought we'd know by January 2012, the year of the London Games, whether we were going on or not. Questions were being asked in the media. Surely, they said, if this is to be a Paralympics about diversity, opportunity and inspiration, you can't dismiss a team that's been training like hell to make their country proud and boost the sport, especially since we had a host national place guaranteed. On the other hand, UK Sport, who would make the final decision, was only too aware they had to demonstrate value for money.

We knew we were far from hopeless but January came and went without an announcement. Then February. Finally in March we received the heart-lifting news that a GB women's sitting volleyball team would represent their country at the Paralympics. That was one obstacle cleared. But here was the next nail-biter. We had no idea which of us, individually, would be selected to be on that team.

Not knowing was agony and accidentally cut-throat. You'd find yourself thinking, Please, please, please make it me, and then realise this was a horrible wish to visit on your mates. It was ruthless. The squad had to be cut down to twelve. You were either in or out. I had about ten tons of emotional baggage riding on this decision.

We couldn't believe how long it was taking. It was the day before the announcement of the Paralympic GB team when Steve, our coach, finally let us know he wanted to see us one by one in the changing room. We knew instantly what that meant. It was a bit like going to a firing squad, but with volleyballs instead of bullets. When it was my turn, I think I stopped breathing until I heard the words, 'You're in, Martine', and then I was flooded with relief.

The next morning we were invited to City Hall on the Thames for the official announcement of the Paralympic team. I was ushered onto a balcony for media interviews and, when they asked how much it meant to me, I pointed to a building directly opposite, next to Tower Bridge, to demonstrate the extraordinary change in my fortunes.

'You see that office block over there,' I said 'That's my old office, on the fifth floor. That's where I was going on the morning of 7/7 when a bomb completely changed the course of my life. I couldn't possibly have dreamed I'd be here now, about to represent the country I love, in the city I love, at my home Paralympics. It's just beyond belief. I'm ecstatic.'

I'd chalked up another coincidence. This wasn't my imagination. I was more and more convinced I was meant to do this.

The next morning, the newspapers carried the names of the squad: Amy Brierly, Andrea Green, Claire

Harvey, Emma Wiggs, Jessica Frezza, Jessica O'Brien, Julie Rogers, Martine Wright, Jodi Hill, Sam Bowen, Vicky Widdup.

In black and white. My name. I'm a Paralympian.

8

'Go Mummy Go!'

I'm sitting on the balcony of our 'penthouse suite' in the Paralympic Village, sipping tea with Claire alongside me. We're gazing down at the most astonishing scene. This is not the Olympic Village any more. It's had a Paralympic makeover. It's a new world. From our perch, eight floors up, I have a bird's eye view. I've never seen so many wheelchairs in one place. Nor prosthetic legs, some attached, some carried, some lying around. There are athletes with dwarfism riding around on kids' bikes.

It's nine o'clock at night. Claire and I look at one another significantly.

'Not home yet, are they?' I say.

'We said nine, didn't we?'

'Give 'em another ten minutes,' I say, remembering my own youthful enthusiasms.

More tea supped in silence. Followed by excited babble heard outside.

'Oh, I can hear 'em. Here they come.'

We were like a couple of old mums, looking out for the young 'uns. In effect, that's what we were. The elders of the team keeping a watchful eye on the youngsters: Jay, now a young mum, and Julie, a 13-year-old and one of the youngest paralympians, being given a taste of Paralympic sport. Claire and I were supposed to be the sensible, steadying influences, while trying to contain the excitement that bubbled up inside us every time we thought, *we are actually here*. Here in the middle of the greatest sporting event this country has ever known.

The word 'unbelievable' gets overworked but this was certainly it. Emotionally I was all over the place. All our hard work had paid off – relief. I'm a Bow bells cockney taking part in the London Paralympics – ecstatic joy. I'm so nervous – terror. Supposing we don't play well enough – fear. How's Nick, Oscar, the family? – anxiety. Oh God, Prince Edward wants to meet us – please, Jay, don't say anything inappropriate.

That's pretty much how the weeks leading up to the Games had proceeded: one big washing machine of churning moods. For a final blast of full-time preparation we went to Loughborough University, one of the country's finest sporting hubs, to live and train six days a week. It was vital for us as a team but I was always torn about Oscar. I felt rushed, stressed and anxious. It's one of the

most important jobs in the world being a mum to a toddler and this felt a bit like absconding. If I wasn't there,
then Nick, Mum, Dad, my sister and Nick's mum and dad
were obviously on duty themselves.

I received phone calls from Nick, sounding stressed out.
'When is all this going to stop?' he'd sometimes say.

'Look, I'll give it up now,' I'd answer.

'No, no, you've got to do it.'

'No, no . . .'

He knew I had to. He wanted me to. But no one knew
better than me that day-to-day combat with toddlerhood
can leave you massively frazzled.

We did a deal. He would support me all the way to the
Paralympics, knowing how much it meant to me, and I
would support him immediately afterwards to do his MA
in photography. So far the non-nuclear treaty was just
about holding.

Nick kept a lot from me. He didn't tell me until after the
event that he'd rushed Oscar to A&E one night with a
rash and a high temperature. He'd rung Mum, he'd tried
Calpol, but, in fear of meningitis, he panicked and
whipped Oscar to the hospital to be safe. It was a false
alarm, thank God. In the end, tonsillitis was diagnosed. If
I'd been there I might have sensed what to do or, at the
very least, I'd have gone to hospital with them. Nick had
his family and my family as support, but it's not the same
thing as having your partner under the same roof.

It was after that he knew he had to make a decision.

One part of him wanted to really give his photography business a go. He'd set it up – weddings and parties mainly – in 2006, and he needed to concentrate on it full-time if he was going to make it a profitable career. Another part of him wanted to support me and my sporting career all the way to the Excel Arena. They were mutually exclusive; he could see that.

He sat himself down one day and just chose. 'Either I'm selfish, and say, "I can't do this. It's impossible. I'm going to put myself and my photography first in this family. She'll have to stop and come home." Or I abandon the business and help Martine focus on something she so wants to do.'

He said, and I believe him, it was very difficult. He felt like he was sharing me with the rest of the world. He'd just wanted to have a nice family when we married, but instead there were a lot of people in this marriage, including a sport and everyone else. He didn't begrudge me. It was just very, very hard. I've since asked him how he decided. He smiles, as if I don't know the answer.

'I couldn't do it. I couldn't, after everything, make a decision that stamped on the dream. You had the opportunity to make something brilliant happen. How could I possibly stand in your way?'

So not much had been going smoothly, either at home or on court. Given our training problems in the run up to the Games, Steve decided we needed a vice captain to help Claire share the load. It made sense. There were more requests from the media for interviews, players had come and gone and the pressure was building. We were beyond the stage of sitting down together for a pow-wow and letting our emotions out. This was serious. We had a sports psychologist who would drum 'positivity' into us. We'd be given newsletters to read on the team bus about a mythical world where the GB women's sitting volley-ball team had scored a brilliant victory over, say, Ukraine. They would personalise it to the extent that Martine Wright would be singled out for her match-winning series smashes. This was great stuff. But it had to trans-late into victory in the real world not just on paper.

British Volleyball were not going to impose the choice on us. It would be up to the team in a secret ballot. It turned out every vote, bar mine, was for me. In the scheme of things it probably doesn't sound like such a big deal. Yet it gave me tremendous reassurance and pride to think that my teammates held me in that kind of esteem. I love being in a team. It has its own dynamic and bonding mechanisms. Maybe they sensed how much it meant to me and how much I wanted to do well for them, myself and – I know this is going to sound cheesy – my country.

After Loughborough we were allowed to go home for about a week, which was wonderful and challenging in equal parts. I remember folding my clothes and packing a suitcase thinking, When these come out again, I'll be at the pre-Paralympic camp at Bath University. Next stop Olympic Park.

The Bath camp had been designed to closet Para-lympians from all the different disciplines and to breed a fighting spirit, a will to win and all those other vital ingredients an athlete needs before the competition of their lives. In fact, it bred germs. We all caught horrendous colds. As we were meant to be supremely fit athletes I could see the funny side.

Of course you couldn't take anything. No Lemsips allowed; just a stick of something up your nose. But we must have been inspired by adversity because on the media day in Bath, when the place was flooded with journalists to do their pre-Paralympics stories, we played a demonstration match – and we were brilliant. What a confidence boost! I'm not sure what was in their nose sticks . . . I'm joking. This was our last chance to get it all together before we were unveiled to the world as part of Paralympics GB, and we'd done it. Everyone was on a high.

Next stop: Stratford. I'm not sure our coach driver knew what he was doing. He went the most peculiar way from Bath to the Olympic Park, right through central London. I started to take this personally. We were on a tour passing some of the most significant addresses of my life. Aldgate tube station, Bart's, The Royal London – how could I not be continually struck that the Paralympics were going to have a profound significance for me?

Seven years ago – that number seven again – I'd been blown up because I'd been to bed late the night before celebrating the successful London bid for the Games. Now I was traveling towards the Olympic Park, not as a spectator but as an athlete – a fully-fledged Paralympic athlete. This wasn't a consolation prize. It didn't feel like that at all. It was vindication, celebration. This was meant to be.

The opening ceremony on 29 August 2012 was a big old night. It had been a mad, mad rush to get ready. We'd had a team meeting that ran so long that we only had about twenty minutes tops to do hair and make-up and get into Stella McCartney's gear, that blinged us up like Ali G. All white and gold. We were all trying to get shoes on that wouldn't fit on our various prosthetic or non-standard feet. Stella hadn't thought about that. We were all cracking up laughing at each other when we met downstairs at the Village.

As hosts, we were due to be last into the stadium during the parade of the teams, so we watched it on a big screen in a 'holding pen', which was actually the on-site GB medical centre. We were continuing to take the mickey out of each other when, all of a sudden, this film came on about me. Channel 4 had made a six-minute video, *The Journey*, of my story. Sean Bean was the narrator (and no, I didn't meet him. Everyone asks that). It was very arty, with music and news footage from the day of the bombing. I was warned they were going to do it. But it was still weird.

'That morning I decided to have ten minutes more in bed,' the huge screen version of me was saying. They cut away to the sight of ambulances and you could hear the voice of a newsreader saying the words 'killing and maiming' over the sound of sirens. Me again: 'I don't remember the pain ... it was getting quieter and quieter ... people were dying.'

There's a close-up of me crying. I try to reassure the camera crew, who want to stop. 'S'all right. S'all right,' I say. 'I just think I'm so lucky ... I knew I had to do something as a result of losing my legs that day otherwise it would all be a complete waste of time.

'Maybe I was always meant to get up late that morning. Maybe I was always meant to run up that escalator and jump on that carriage. Maybe I was always meant to do this journey. All I can say is that I'm just lucky to be living this dream now.'

It was very, very moving for me to see it and yet I'm also thinking, Oh shut up, Martine! That's enough. Luckily my teammates offered wisecracks all the way through to distract me from the thought that this film was beaming round the world to billions. It opened a real mixed bag of feelings. Wow, that's me, followed by, Oh God, that's me. It was uncomfortable. It was pressure. It was a source of pride. All those things rolled up together. Ultimately it made me reflective. It reminded me where I'd been, what I'd been through, what my family had been through beside me.

Lining up in the tunnel ready to enter the stadium was thrilling. But the queue moved desperately slowly. Pigeon steps. Pigeon wheels in my case, as I'd opted for my chair. Tension was building. The crowd was roaring. Clare Balding was there at the entrance to the stadium to do a quick interview. I think I made sense but who knows. As I was answering her questions the rest of the team behind me were untunefully singing 'There's Only One Clare Balding...'

Lights were flashing everywhere as we emerged into view. The decibel level was ridiculous. People were going bonkers, waving flags as confetti cascaded down from the roof. I found myself manically waving with both hands. I thought my arms were going to fly off I was waving so hard. What am I doing? I tried to ask myself but there was just no stopping it.

As the GB women's sitting volleyball team, we'd never played before a crowd of more than 500. Here was 80,000 screaming for us. It was a very, very special night, and so much for turning off your phones for the duration of the Games; I got millions of texts. It was fabulous. It was one of the biggest and best nights of my life.

We got back to our penthouse really late and totally wired. There was only one thing for it. Claire and I sent 'the kids' to bed and sat on the balcony with a cup of tea, reliving it all and trying to calm down. Tomorrow we'd be training in Bexleyheath and the next day we'd play our first match – against Ukraine. One of the best teams in the world.

*

It was an early morning match at the Excel Arena in Greenwich. We were up at the crack of dawn. My family was up even earlier. About six months previously they'd bought up all these Paralympic day passes to the Excel Arena – you don't get free tickets for your family when you're a Paralympian – not knowing whether I'd be playing or not. It was a gamble but they weren't going to miss their daughter/sister/wife/mum performing at the greatest show on earth.

The rules of the day pass were that you'd be allowed in to watch the matches but with no specific seat. Their plan was to get there so early that they could sit together in one big block. It was a massive morning for them. They left home at 5.30 a.m. Mum, Dad, Maureen, Nick, Oscar, Grant, Tracey, Alicia, Tyler and Lewis, plus my physio Maggie, loads of friends and all my NCT mates from Tring. Families of Paralympians had explicit instructions not to contact you before your event. I had minute-by-minute text updates from mine: 'Leaving now'. 'A40 not too bad'. 'So excited'. 'Love you'. 'Good luck'.

I tried to imagine what it would be like to see them all when I appeared on court, and then I tried not to because the thought was overwhelming. I still didn't know whether I'd been selected to start the match. We'd only be told on the warm-up court beforehand. This was really hard. I'd been upset at other tournaments leading up to this because the coach had a habit of subbing me on and off. Only six players are allowed on the court at any one time and naturally the best players tend to spend longer out there. The rest sit on the bench waiting for their moment. I'd done plenty of that.

To be fair to Steve, our coach, he'd taken me aside at one point and explained that I had a unique skill set that he valued very highly.

'You're so mentally strong that you can handle being subbed on and off much better than some of the other girls.'

It may have been motivational bullshit but I chose to believe it and it helped get me through.

Anyway, I had other things to think about. Not least my 'second wee'. Most sportspeople have their superstitions: putting socks on in a certain order or wearing a special bit of kit. I didn't have any of that. I just had to have two wees before a match – one just before warm-up on the practice court and one just before the match started – and if I didn't then I'd be thinking about it all game.

This was a big thing for me. My deepest concern at this iconic pre-match moment was not playing for my country in front of my beloved family and millions of other people watching at home on TV; it was actually, how the hell am I going to get my second wee in?

I knew I'd be in the Excel Arena by then, and I'd need to go through about four or five checkpoints with my accreditation just to get to the nearest loo. It would mean flying along in my wheelchair about 30 m.p.h. to get there and back in time. It was a big worry. Even for the girls. This was tense stuff.

The first wee was accomplished no problem. When I returned Steve called us all over.

'This is our starting six ...' He read out the names. Mine wasn't on it. 'Martine, you're on the bench.'

Shit. I was disappointed, but I couldn't afford to let it show to the other girls. We were being gathered together in the tunnel to go out in front of the crowd. It reminded me of the scenes you see at football matches when the players line up, studiously avoiding the camera up their nose, with that faraway look in their eyes.

That tunnel was like the twilight zone. An underground world, dim fluorescent lights, the echo of the on-court announcer reverberating around us. I held my breath. 'OK, time to go,' someone said. Suddenly I was wheeling myself towards the brightness and the clamour of 3,000 people going mad. Using a wheelchair was my choice. I prefer it to wearing my legs. Some volleyballers do and then take them off by the side of the court to be wheeled away in shopping trollies. That would be too much bother. The joy of the sport is the sense of freedom it gives you.

I spotted my family immediately. It was Dad's banner that naturally caught my attention. It was huge: 'Good Luck GB Volleyball Girls!' and one of the letters was backwards. Oh, there you go. That's my dad, I thought. I didn't know how the people behind them were going to watch the match, given that they were half-obscured by the banner. 'SLIMMING WORLD!' Later when I looked up, the words on the banner had bizarrely changed to 'Sign Up Today! First Week Free!' What? Then it dawned on me: he'd nicked the banner, hadn't he? From the British Legion, which had been holding some slimmers' do the week before. Thought he'd save himself some money, take it home and write his message on the back. Obviously, with all the excitement, he'd got it twisted round.

Now Mum was bawling her eyes out. Nick was holding Oscar, who held up a sign saying 'Go Mummy Go!'. I swallowed hard to keep the emotion in. I knew how much this meant to me, would always mean to me, but I had a job to do on the court. Right now I was an athlete who could tolerate no distractions, but who was I kidding . . . this scene, this moment, was a wonderful message to the people I loved. Here am I, seven years after something so hugely negative, with my three-year-old son holding up a banner in my name and my whole family and friends going crazy. This was me, saying to them: 'Actually, it's not too bad, is it, life now? We've been through the tough times and now it's OK.'

I hit a few practice balls over the net, then resolutely put my hand up. Time for the second wee. I must have broken some kind of wheelchair record, held by Tanni Grey-Thompson, probably, for speed to the nearest toilet and back. Slightly breathless but relieved, I took my place on the bench where I led the cheerleading from the sidelines. We lost the first set conclusively 25–9 but we were playing well in the second. We were holding them back, almost matching them hit for hit. That's when Steve indicated he wanted me on. I took off my tracksuit top. Then the stadium announcer did his thing.

'And now, coming on, number seven, Martine WRIGHT,' as I shuffled on my bum into place on court. I wasn't prepared for the reaction.

It seemed as though all 3,000 people were cheering. It's the first time I felt bewildered. This was my first connection with the outside world for weeks. I hadn't realised the hype. They were shouting my name. I looked up to see all these banners with 'Martine' on them. Not just my family but strangers. I categorically had no idea there would be this kind of reception.

I refused to let myself be overwhelmed by it. The Ukrainians, tall, powerful, organised, would be a match for anyone and we, the absolute underdogs, were so close to keeping up with them. It was so tight, so tense. Their lead had been reduced to just two points. They won the second set 25–20. It would all go down to the third and deciding set.

I couldn't help but look around in the break. The audience was crazy. They'd been warmed up beforehand by the unlikely double act of Boris Johnson, then London Mayor, and Barbara Windsor, the formidable Peggy from *EastEnders*. Apart from matching hairdos they didn't seem to have much in common except the desire to get the crowd going. We'd met them briefly in the warm-up zone. Barbara had that proper cockney thing, where she grips your hand and looks you in the eye. I liked her.

The Ukrainians won in straight sets in the end, but we were encouraged; we hadn't embarrassed ourselves or our country. We'd fought as hard as we could. We came off the court sweating, exhausted, but not unhappy, and were told we could go to a reserved area behind the stand to meet our friends and family. I was overjoyed. I so wanted to see everybody, especially Oscar, and give him a huge hug.

My God, it was a frenzy out there. Never mind friends and family. There seemed to be half of the Olympic Park in there: cameras, photographers, journalists, lights in my face. Oscar was in my lap, giving me a cuddle. Mum was beside me. Nick was lurking somewhere. One of my natural childbirth mates in Tring was saying, 'Oh, Martine, that was amazing, but next time we're not going to sit behind your family.'

'Oh God, why not?' I asked, fearing they'd done something to show themselves up.

'Because we couldn't see anything from behind your dad's banner!'

I laughed. Yeah, but they might have joined Slimming World. He should get commission.

It was there, during the mayhem, that Oscar turned to me and said, 'Mummy not play volleyball any more. Mummy come home.'

My heart turned over. For a split second I thought, I can't do this. I'm going home. Every time I left this little boy it was a huge emotional wrench and now he was begging me to stop. Even with the cameras in front of me there were tears pouring down my face. I tried to get some kind of grip.

I expect I said something like, 'Don't worry, Oscar. I won't be for much longer. Daddy will look after you,' and all those other platitudes that cut no ice with a toddler who wants his mum. I knew I couldn't just abandon the team and the wider impact it was having on me. Obviously I was about to go off again. We had two more matches in our group: Holland and Japan. Both were ranked higher than us. We had to win to go further in the tournament. We had to concentrate on ourselves. But I was feeling hugely guilty.

Oscar was prised off my lap by Nick in the end and the hectic scramble closed with me trying to kiss and say goodbye to about a hundred people. Then it was back to the surreal world of the Paralympic Village, submerging again in the bubble.

My family went home on the tube in a state of high excitement. They told me all about it later. Someone in their carriage was reading an *Evening Standard*. It had a huge picture of me on the front. Tyler nudged his mum.

'There's Martine,' he said in amazement. You can't activate someone like Tracey and not expect everyone to hear about it.

'That's my sister,' she announced to the innocent reader. Within seconds the whole carriage was in uproar chatting about the Paralympics in general and my sporting debut in particular.

I was blissfully ignorant of all this. It seemed highly unlikely that a straight-sets defeat would make the media headlines when there were so many gold medals and stunning performances to celebrate. It didn't cross my mind that it would. So I was truly astonished the next morning when I bumped into someone who said I was all over the front pages of the daily newspapers: 'A poignant symbol of recovery and courage'.

That made me proud. Being so concerned with my own personal quest, I hadn't realised the effect on the outside world. I wanted what had happened to me to mean something positive. That's why I noticed all those coincidences. They were signposts to me, not just a bunch of happy accidents. Old memories could hurt, so I was overlaying them with new ones that brought me happiness instead. If I didn't do something positive my survival would have been a complete waste of time. Somewhere down the line, the Paralympic dream had become my personal dream come true.

All the wishing in the world, though, couldn't conjure a win for the team, which would have been the ultimate excitement. What we had done was extraordinary – the first Paralympic team to be started from scratch and appear at a Paralympics in the space of two years. But in the pressurised glare of world-class competition we were not battle-hardened nor united enough to achieve a precious win. We tried, *we really tried*, but we were probably still a bunch of enthusiastic individuals trying to mould ourselves into a team.

Three defeats in the round robin stage signalled our departure from the competition. I have the lingering feeling that at our best we really could have beaten Japan, and the mood in the locker room afterwards was initially depressed. But we rallied. I did anyway. To me it was the most moving, life-changing, wonderful experience I'd ever know – win, lose or draw. We'd have a few days now to decompress, celebrate Jodi's birthday – Claire sneaked out of the Village for a hedgehog cake – and take in the vastness of the Paralympic dining hall.

Next up was the closing ceremony. Before I squeezed into Stella's mad shoes that didn't fit one more time, I made a visit to the Olympic Village hairdresser, which Claire kindly booked for me. I arrived at the salon and the very sweet girl behind the counter, checking her appointment book, said, 'Yeah, Martine Wright, we've got you down for a cut and blow dry – and a pedicure.'

The ceremony itself had a much more relaxed feel than the opening version. By now we'd swapped Ali G for blue blazers and red jodhpurs. We didn't march in as a country but Claire and I rolled in together in our wheelchairs and headed for the stage where Rihanna was going to play. In keeping with the fractured relationships that had existed in the team, Emma and Andrea made for the Coldplay stage. I would have loved to have spent the night as a team together but I didn't worry about that any more. I was looking around for my sister and Tyler somewhere in the crowd, since I'd managed to get them two tickets through Channel 4. Amazingly I saw them and was so excited I yelled up at them. About a hundred people sitting all around them yelled 'Martine!' back. Blimey. How did they know who I was?

That set my sister off. Now she's yelling, 'Martine!' at me, and, 'That's my sister!' at everyone in the seats beside her. This went on for some time.

It was an amazing end to the event, but when it started pouring with rain and the plastic macs were being handed out I decided I just wanted it to be over so I could relax over a beer with my teammates. Actually I had a choice to make. It was midnight and I'd been invited to ParaGB House – a building close by that had been dolled up to look after us and host interviews with the media – for the after-Games party. I'd looked in earlier that day to meet a journalist and heard the strains of Spandau Ballet's famous: 'Gold, always believe in your soul . . .' I loved Tony Hadley. Then I turned a corner and it *was* Tony Hadley.

So the choice was champagne, fun, party and 'Gold, always believe . . . etc,' or the barbecue area of the Paralympic Village surrounded by boxes of condoms and a flow of warm beer with the girls. Village won and I proceeded to get very drunk. We didn't get to bed until around 4.30 a.m. and we had to be up and ready three hours later for a police escort to the Guildhall. This was for the grand finale – the open-top bus parade through London.

The first person I met was Tom Daly and I took the opportunity to give him a big hug, hoping that the after-fumes of beer had worn off by now. The athletes were loaded onto the specially decorated buses – it felt a bit like American tourists doing the capital – and we set off. I'd loved the opening and closing ceremonies but this was the most emotional event of the lot.

I stood on the upper deck of the bus and watched London slowly reel by. The iconic monuments I knew so well as kid from our car rides to Old Street to visit my nan: Tower Bridge, the Tower of London, the Monument. Just seeing the Monument brought back all those times when, as a kid, Dad took me up those 311 stone steps to the top where you could look down at the site in Pudding Lane where the Great Fire of London started. It was so poignant. Of the whole Paralympics, the parade was, for me, the most emotional event of them all.

Every street and mews and alleyway was packed with thousands of people cheering and waving at us. They were standing along the route all the way to Trafalgar Square, hundreds deep, with builders waving from scaffolding and office workers hanging out of windows. Loads of people were shouting 'Martine'. A bloke held up a baby dressed in a union flag babygrow. I laughed and waved.

This was my London, going nuts with happiness and celebration. What a grand finale!

Clare Balding found me and gave me a hug while I tried not to breathe old beer fumes over her. We did an interview which I really hope made sense. The chances of it being audible were probably slim over the din and the Red Arrow's fly-past with their red, white and blue jet stream. Then Iwan Thomas, the former GB athlete, joined me on the bus for another interview. He asked me that old favourite question: how was I feeling? I immediately became emotional talking about my family and coming back to London to be part of something so magical after my previous experience. He just ended up cuddling me while I cried on his shoulder with the camera still rolling.

Going back to the Paralympic Village felt weird. Lovely flats but I just wanted to go home now. I called Nick to come and get me. He couldn't drive through the security cordon, so I arranged to meet him at Stratford station. It was quite a hike from my flat and, as I had so overloaded my bag with everything that wasn't nailed down in our rooms – duvet, towels, water bottles – I needed assistant coach Karen to help me lug it over. It was packed to bursting, like the one Mary Poppins owned, only minus the ornamental hat stand.

Puffing and pulling we made it to the station and I felt pure relief when I saw Nick standing there.

'Take me home,' I said.

9

Fame Academy

I loved watching *SPOTY*, the BBC's *Sports Personality of the Year* show. Being a massive sports fan, I've always enjoyed that irresistible combination of action clips, chats with the stars and household arguments about who should win. I can remember all the way back to the days of Kenny Dalglish and Kevin Keegan (big favourites of mine, despite the rest of the family supporting Arsenal), Seb Coe, Steve Cram, Sally Gunnell. Huge, huge stars. As remote to my life as the planet Pluto.

I never, ever dreamed I would be on the show. The day I was phoned and told that, not only would I be appearing on the 2012 celebration of the Olympics and Paralympics, but that I was also going to be presented with the Helen Rollason Award for 'outstanding achievement in the face of adversity', was bordering on the surreal. The obvious thing to do was to call Mum and Dad and stand by for screaming. But the BBC had sworn me to secrecy unless I could completely trust my confidantes to say nothing. That ruled out my entire family (bar Nick) straightaway. I had to keep the news to myself. It was agony! Named after one of the BBC's pioneering female sports presenters who died of cancer in 1999, the award is highly prestigious. This was going to be a huge honour. And terrifying.

I had an agent by now – a novelty I wasn't yet used to. The idea of me coming out with the Hollywood phrase, 'Speak to my agent' sounded mad, but so many requests for appearances and talks were coming in that I needed the help. A household with a toddler and me in it tended to lose pieces of paper with telephone messages on them. So when Martin and Helen came on board some structure was imposed on my disorganised life.

The 2012 version of *SPOTY* was being held in London, of course, not far from the Olympic Stadium. Nick came with me to the hotel beforehand and an entire gang of my family was making its own way there. It was like a rerun of the Paralympics themselves: me getting into an anxious state and them coming along to make a racket.

It was truly nerve-jangling. I had done one TED Talk, with a distinct quiver in my voice as I started (although I finished a bit more confidently), but this was taking things to a whole new level. The organisers had given us a room in a nearby hotel to relax in before the event. Relax? Every time Nick tried to say something encouraging I told him to shut up – as nicely as possible, of course. I was trying to learn a speech because there were so many things I wanted to say.

'I'm sorry, but you mustn't talk to me for the next hour-and-a-half while I concentrate,' I said, romantically.

By the time we went in for the rehearsal I was even more nervous. I was wearing my legs and determined I'd walk onto the stage unaided apart from my stick. It was quite a distance when I saw it for the first time and, naturally, there was a ramp to negotiate.

'Right, let's give it a go, Martine,' said the stage manager, planning a run-through. 'We've made a mark on the stage. That's where you've got to stop.'

I set off. It's the nature of C-Legs that you have to swing from the hips to move forward, with the result that you accelerate as you go along. Plus I needed momentum to get up the ramp. It was like Mount Everest to me. By the time I was on the stage I was flying. I shot past the mark and only managed to come to a halt halfway to the wings on the other side.

'Oh,' said the stage manager. 'Can you slow down a bit?'

'Not really,' I replied, fearing I'd get stuck halfway up the ramp.

'OK,' he said brightly. 'We'll move your mark further back.'

A reception was held before the show, to which Mum,

Dad, Maureen, Tracey, Tyler and Lissy all had access because of their VIP invitations. I thought they might twig about the award, since they were steered onto the red carpet and walked in alongside Mo Farah and Jess Ennis. But no. Dad was more preoccupied by taking photos with an old-school camera.

'Go on, Martina [Navratilova], stand next to Martine – that's right. Lovely. Give us a big smile.' He was having a whale of a time.

Soon we were all ushered through to the theatre. The lights dimmed, music swelled and the show began. Blimey, not long now. I noticed I'd have to walk right past my family when the time came to go up on stage. No way could I look at them; that would set me off. So when Gary Lineker introduced the Helen Rollason Award, I set my eyes firmly on the stage and kept walking, while an interview they'd previously filmed with me was playing. A few words were filtering through, as I concentrated on putting one bionic leg in front of the other.

'Suddenly I saw this figure coming towards me,' I heard myself say.

Then: 'Her left leg was sort of squashed against the side of the train and her right leg was mostly blown away.'

I recognised that voice, it was Liz Kenworthy. And when I looked up there she was, standing next to Denise Lewis to help present my award. I could feel the emotion building seeing her there. I didn't realise until I watched it later that everyone in the audience was standing up applauding and (in the case of the Wrights) cheering. Probably just as well. I think that would have finished me off before I even gave my speech.

I hit my mark OK, following my trek across the stage, received a kiss from Gary Lineker, and then Liz gave me the biggest hug and a smile. It was wonderful to see her. It was going to be well-nigh impossible to remember everything I wanted to say, and I could hear my voice shaking, but I gave it a go.

I thanked everyone who'd supported me to get this far: Liz, for saving my life, and the emergency services and medical staff who had done so much that day and going forward. I said I would never forget the fifty-two who'd lost their lives and that I considered the award very much for them and their families too. I thanked the athletes and the volunteers – the Games Makers, who had been so fantastic throughout the summer. Finally I thanked the whole of Great Britain for its support and spirit. 'Let's build on this legacy,' I said, and I meant every word. Incredibly, miraculously, I got through the whole thing without crying.

Job not quite done yet. Afterwards I joined a panel discussion on Radio 5 live with James Cracknell, the Olympic rower. Then I was ushered to a small room to speak to the press.

'I'm not being funny,' I said, before I sat down, 'but I need a drink. I'm parched.' I looked at the group of journalists. 'And could you all not say I was swigging it as we spoke.' Bless them, they didn't.

That was it. I was ready to join the party by then, but there was one more surprise. A member of the crew came up and asked, 'Would you like to join Clare Balding for a moment in the VIP marquee? She's going to introduce you to the Duchess of Cambridge.' This was getting more extraordinary by the moment.

So now I'm meeting the duchess, who is asking polite questions, and all I can think is, Blimey, I know your uncle. He used to ply me with peach schnapps when I worked for his company.

I tried to quell this terrible urge but found myself blurting out: 'I've got to tell you that your sister, Pippa–' as though she didn't know who her sister was '–she used to work with me at the IT Job Board. Martine WRIGHT. And my friend, Alex OGDEN.'

I'm by now talking slowly and deliberately, as you would to someone slightly deaf. Oh, God. Make me stop.

'Say hello to her for me, won't you?'

She said, probably alarmed, that she would.

This massive embarrassment was fortunately covered by Martina Navratilova losing the heel of her shoe and everyone running around trying to find a matching replacement.

The cast list of great athletes was incredible. Tyler, my nephew, was ecstatic to meet Jess Ennis and Kelly Holmes. His joy was complete when Kelly later re-tweeted one of his tweets.

I met someone very special, too, when Helen Rollason's

daughter Nikki came and introduced herself and thanked me for the speech. She didn't have to do that, and I was exceptionally touched that she had gone out of her way to make the connection. I could see why her mum had been so proud of her and she had been so proud of her mum.

The entire afterparty was a whirl. Nick, Mum, Dad, the rest of the family, adrenalin, relief, celebration, red wine, Bradley Wiggins (before the Sir happened) playing guitar on stage. We all had a fantastic time and it carried on for Nick and I when we popped into the bar of our hotel for one final snifter. There was a crowd already in there, including Jess Ennis, Steve Cram and Paula Radcliffe. It would have been rude not to go over and say hello. We had a marvellous time, although I still owe Jess the money for my bar bill, especially as my husband was drinking Woodford Reserve bourbon!

Nick found all this a lot harder than I did. Chatting to strangers, especially famous strangers, has never been his idea of fun. I used to say, 'Relax, lighten up,' which he sometimes construed as, 'Have a few drinks.'

Nick decided early on in the process that for the sake of his wellbeing and sanity it was probably better he took a back seat. 'I'm just an ordinary bloke,' he'd say. 'I don't really want to get drunk and find myself photo-bombing Bradley Wiggins.'

'You were chatting well enough to Jess Ennis's dad,' I'd remind him.

'Yeah, but that's only because I didn't know who he was. If I do, I get star-struck and clam up.'

He once tutted at Roy Hodgson, though, the ex-England football manager, for using a disabled lift, which was quite brave of him. But he didn't know who Roy was at the time. He's one of those blokes who until he knows you seems quite shy. He reckons it's partly because he has dyslexia and didn't have a lot of confidence growing up. So I don't pester him to come to loads of things with me. It works. He doesn't have to come along to get nervous and I don't have to worry about him feeling agitated in the presence of celebrities.

So, apart from Nick feeling awkward, *SPOTY* had been a big success. Although for days afterwards I spoke to people who said, 'Saw you on *Sports Personality*. Very good, but my God didn't they make you walk a long way!'

I didn't explain it was my fault.

I was still far from sure I had any career going forward. I'd been in the marketing world for years and I knew the public speaking industry was overloaded already. I've seen some bad speakers; we all have. I didn't want to be one of them. Even though I'd done lots of press and TV in the lead-up to and during the Paralympics, I was nowhere near your slick, PowerPointed-up corporate speaker. I was much more down to earth and normal. Was there any kind of market for me? When Martin said, 'You're really good at it,' was he just massaging my ego?

I had genuine doubts but it was becoming urgent that I start to earn money, as Nick had by now embarked on his MA course. I wanted to live up to my promise after all the compromises he'd made to help get me to the Paralympics. I was going to have to be the main breadwinner. But how?

Enquiries started coming in, albeit slowly at first. Would I attend an event here, give a talk there? It grew steadily, which surprised me. Usually there's a rush of enthusiasm for athletes to speak immediately after an Olympics and Paralympics, then it starts to tail off as the fame inevitably dwindles. But I was lucky. I had, in a sense, a two-tiered story. Yes, I had been a Paralympian but I also had the tale of 7/7 to tell. Being part of a day everyone remembers –where they were, what they saw, who they tried to get hold of – has allowed me to have an emotional connection to an audience, which can be a rare and difficult thing for a speaker to achieve.

People to this day come up to me after a talk and say, 'I remember what happened on 7/7.' 'Oh, I was late that morning as well,' or 'I was two trains behind.' They want to hear about it and share the experience. I realised I was putting one of my greatest natural talents – talking a lot – to use in a way I couldn't have predicted.

I took it seriously. I'd spend hours and hours down the bottom of my garden in Nick's office with my laptop, surrounded by a mountain of screwed-up paper, deciding 'this works; that doesn't work', until I had a working script. I'd recite it out loud over and over again – first reading it and then remembering it without looking. I didn't cry then. I was concentrating. But I still cannot watch the part where I'm crying in *The Journey*. I often show it during a presentation and I just have to look down at my feet – well, not my *feet*, obviously, but you know what I mean – until that part is over. There's another film, made by the BBC, called *One Day*, which I know was very good. I've hardly watched that either. I'm not sure I ever will. I've never really watched a documentary I've been in.

Before I lost my legs I was very career-hungry. I felt pressure to succeed, being the first one in the family to go to university and have a City job. But by this time, 2012 and beyond, I had changed. I was much more laid back. I didn't – I still don't – have a five-year plan or a ten-year plan, which really winds up my husband. I just enjoy what I do and hope it lasts.

'What can you see yourself doing in two years' time, babe?' Nick will say to me.

'I don't know. I'll just carry on doing what I'm doing as long as it lasts. It might not last forever. See what happens.'

Luckily things carried on happening. In the summer of 2013 Nick and I were invited to the Queen's garden party at Buckingham Palace. Mum and Dad, of course, were gagging to come too but I had only one spare ticket so, rather than upset one of them, Nick was the safer bet. This was a first for us both. I had all sorts of unsolicited advice: I'd have to wear a hat; you've got to take a shawl. But you can't do hats and shawls with a wheelchair. It would be chaos. So I chose to wear my formal black Paralympic trouser suit and, instead of a hat, I had a tan, which is my favourite accessory of choice.

All was going swimmingly well. We met Claire there and you could see quite a few members of the royal family mingling with guests. It was my first brush with royalty since showing Princess Diana round a memorial garden when I was a schoolgirl at Mill Hill High. She was a lovely lady. I found it very easy to chat to her.

While I was talking to Claire at the back of the Palace garden, we suddenly became aware of a man standing beside us, waiting for a gap in the conversation. It's pretty rare that I have gaps in conversation, so we stopped for a minute in case it was important news.

'Hello, ladies,' he said charmingly. 'I wonder if I could have a chat with you. You're Paralympians, aren't you? And what sport do you do? The reason I'm asking is that the Princess Royal was wondering whether she could come over and have a chat.'

We made all the right polite noise and Princess Anne, who had competed in the Olympics herself in 1976, came over and we had a great discussion about sport. She asked me at one point, 'Do you think sport healed you?' I said yes and meant it.

But I suddenly became aware that Claire's attention was wandering. Her eyes were sliding about peculiarly and her head was tilted away from Princess Anne, as though she was trying to peer round her. Something was obviously up. She's normally so correct and professional. She was trying to mouth something secretly to me, but I'm no expert at lip-reading. I was trying to surreptitiously mouth back, 'What? *What?*', aware that royalty was talking to us. As soon as Princess Anne moved on, I said, 'What the hell are you doing?'

'Look behind you,' she practically screamed with excitement. 'It's *Floella Benjamin!*'

'Oh, my God!' Now I was equally excited. 'Not *Floella Benjamin!*'

To children of the 1980s, Floella Benjamin was practically royalty herself. She was absolutely front and centre of our childhoods, as one of the presenters of *Play School*, the BBC kids' show that we watched every day, twice a day, for years. We charged towards her in our wheelchairs, our version of the chariot scene in *Ben Hur*. We both talked at once when we reached her.

'We loved you on *Play School* . . . you look amazing . . . you don't look any older than you did thirty years ago . . . we were just talking to royalty but to be honest we're more excited about you.' She laughed, fortunately.

Afternoon tea was then served, a box containing sandwiches and a drink, and then those in wheelchairs were lined up on the gravel path for the departure of the attending members of the royal family. It's one of the perks of being a wheelchair user that you always seem to get a prime position, and here we were again, in the front row, right next to the palace's indoor swimming pool. While we waited, Claire and I imagined the royals, after a long day, jumping into the pool with all their inflatable toys.

One by one they walked past. The Duke of Edinburgh looked very upright and impressive. Then the Queen came along. I didn't expect her to talk to anyone at this stage, and was far more engaged in trying to take selfies, which you are absolutely forbidden to do. Claire and I were laughing when Her Majesty came up to us.

'Have you enjoyed the day?' she asked.

I immediately split into two parts. One part was thinking: OMG, the Queen is talking to me. The other part just wanted to touch her face and say, 'You really remind me of my Auntie Peggy.' But even in the heat of this particular moment I realised the second option might be inappropriate and I'd never be invited to anything again.

Answer her, answer her, my brain was telling me. Followed by the panic-struck thought of What do I call her? I wasn't prepared for this.

'It's been wonderful, Your Majesty,' I blurted out.

I thought that would be it. But no.

'And how have you found getting around?' I presumed she meant by wheelchair.

'It's been fine, Your Majesty.' Oh no, you're not supposed to call her Your Majesty twice.

And that's when she came up with a line that you really couldn't have guessed in a million years.

'Because this stuff–' she gestured to the gravel '–is awful, isn't it? Awful.'

Did she say 'stuff'? Maybe not. Perhaps 'surface', but my overheated brain couldn't take it all in.

Having dropped that bombshell, she walked on.

I was strongly tempted to shout after her, 'You need to get bigger stones next time, not small ones.' I didn't though.

Prince Andrew then went past, followed by his two daughters. He just strode by, but his eldest, Beatrice, was very professional.

'Oh, I hear you're Paralympians. Oh, I so loved the Paralympics. Didn't we do well . . .'

Eugenie, the younger daughter, was just about to open her mouth to join in when she looked down and practically screamed in amazement.

'Oh! You've got GOLD Converse. Where did you get them from?'

These were my special garden party trainers.

'Er, I got them off the internet,' I said, and told her which website to look for.

'Oh, they look wonderful. I've never seen that colour before . . .' and she charged off, very likely to browse the website in question.

The people I meet are the most fascinating thing about this career I've embarked upon. I don't mind speaking from a stage; I like it. It doesn't rack me with nerves any more. But I love getting to talk to individual people before and afterwards as well. Obviously getting to know Boris Johnson was memorable. As London Mayor immediately after the Paralympics, he invited me to do a talk at City Hall to promote London's new volunteering programme. I was given the working title 'Champion Ambassador for London'.

I met Babs again, Barbara Windsor, who was the Ambassador for Street Parties. What a great title. I was half inclined to ask her to swap but decided you can't beat being a 'champion'. I was intrigued to meet Boris again but clearly this was a high-powered event with MDs and CEOs of major companies like British Airways and Starbucks sprinkled throughout the audience. The Mayoral staff had been very strict with us. The agenda ran something like:

8.01 Martine to arrive
8.02 Martine to be served croissants and coffee
8.04 Martine to take her seat
8.05 Mayor to arrive and look at his notes
8.08 Mayor to introduce the campaign
8.10 Mayor to introduce Martine

Everything went fine until 8.08. That was the moment Boris turned from his notes, ran a distracted hand through his trademark hair, peered up at his audience and started speaking entirely off-piste. A number of his team in the front row put their head in their hands. I can't remember the exact time I did my talk; I just know it wasn't 8.10. I've worked with him many times now and it's always the same.

I was starting to love all this: speaking, meeting, chatting, laughing. Occasionally crying on stage, too, when blindsided by a memory. People were lovely when that happened. They let me talk myself through it or take a few moments to gather myself and then we were off again. As time went by, my nerves settled down. I was beginning to assume that not much would faze me. Always a fatal thought.

Martin gave me a call to say he'd had a request from Save the Children, who were hosting a volunteer campaign with Virgin called WE Day. 'Fine,' I said. This was familiar territory.

'Where is it?'

'Wembley.'

'What, one of the hotels there?'

'No, the Arena.'

'What, one of the corporate lounges?'

'No, the actual Arena. On stage. In the Arena.'

Oh. The Arena – where some of the biggest bands in the world have played. Where I've seen Madonna and Robbie Williams and where I took my niece, Lissy, to see the Pussycat Dolls. That Arena. I realised I hadn't entirely got over my nerves after all.

I couldn't blag this one. I was going to have to be one

hundred per cent prepared. I learned my speech inside and out. I made sure my kit was all ironed. I had an early night beforehand. Everything was as perfect as I could make it. I woke up the next morning, dressed, put on my legs and discovered that one of the chargers hadn't worked overnight. Oh no. No, no, no, no. I knew from experience that this would mean I wouldn't be able to bend my knee. I was about to play Wembley Arena with the pronounced limp of Long John Silver.

There was nothing else for it. Later, with a deep breath, I hobbled onto the world-famous stage looking not unlike John Cleese doing his famous 'silly walk' from *Monty Python's Flying Circus*. On the way to the lectern I passed Jennifer Hudson, the American singer/actress, who smiled and drawled, 'Good luck, Martine.'

Oh, my God. This was a seriously high-profile event organised by Holly Branson, Richard Branson's daughter, and packed with star names like Jennifer and singer Ellie Goulding. And here's me with eight minutes to fill, a dodgy leg and a serious case of nerves.

I didn't plan it. But when I reached the middle and looked out at that sea of 9,000 faces through the dazzle of the spotlight, a wicked thought came into my head: I have only have one chance to do this in my entire lifetime, so I'm going to do it now. A silence fell. I inhaled as deeply as I could and then, at the top of my lungs, screamed: 'HELLOOO WEMBLEY!' The place went wild. Thank God. A dream come true.

My performance at the O2 a few months later was completely different. By now these rock concert settings were slightly less alarming, although sitting in the meeting to discuss the event designed to entertain 13,000 accountants still had its outlandish moments.

'So, Lenny Henry will be hosting,' said one of the organisers.

'Sir Bob Geldof will be speaking . . .'

'Jamie Oliver . . .'

'And rapper Tinie Tempah will be performing a couple of his songs . . .'

I was mixing in some seriously famous circles. It made me laugh when I arrived on the day, decanting from a minibus with my wheelchair while Tinie (who isn't tiny) unfolded himself from a ginormous limo. I still have the pictures on my phone of the dressing room doors. 'Sir Bob Geldof' with a big star under it. 'Jamie Oliver' ditto. The next one along: 'Martine Wright' – and my star was as big as theirs.

It wasn't really my world. I knew that. My real world was at home with Oscar and Nick, doing the school run, listening to them babbling on about Obi-Wan Kenobi. Seeing the family, having the girls round, having a beer or a glass of wine, staying close to the people I loved.

But I did enjoy the variety of what you could loosely call my new career. I've been presented with two honorary doctorates, each one very memorable although they could not be more different. One from my old University of East

London, alongside Jamie Oliver's mate, Jimmy Doherty, and the other from York University, presented in the magnificent setting of the cathedral, York Minster. The Archbishop John Sentamu and I became great friends while I was there. He is such a lovely, funny man with an amazing back story, having been born in Uganda, the sixth of thirteen children, then later being beaten up by the country's dictator, Idi Amin, and ultimately thrown out of the country.

I may or may not have told John, as he asked me to call him, that attending church hasn't figured hugely in my life, but I do believe in something like a higher presence without having the slightest idea what it is. I like churches, though, and find something peaceful and comforting about them. I went to a lot of trouble to get christened in my thirties, when I wanted to be godmother to my niece, Matilda.

I was touched that Alley and Grant would want me to be godmother and, although Mum and Dad had never had me christened, which ruled it out, I'd find a way. I went to this church around the corner from me and explained to Father Patrick that even though I was slightly older than the babies he usually met at the font, I'd like to be baptised all the same. I was living and working in London at the time, often clubbing till 6 a.m., but I figured I could fit it in one morning.

'How long will it take to organise?' I asked.

'Well,' said Father Patrick, 'if you attend regularly and

learn everything that needs to be learned, I think we'll be about ready in nine months.'

I gulped. Nine months! That was a pregnancy not a christening. I didn't say that.

He saw the horror-stricken look on my face.

'There are other churches where you can just book in and go,' he said. That was more like it. I fled that scene and phoned the church he mentioned.

'Yes, no problem,' came the good news. Where did I live? I told them. 'Oh, bad luck. You're just out of the area. Have you tried Father Patrick?'

So every Sunday morning I would get up, leaving Nick in bed, saying the unlikely words: 'See you later. I'm off to church.'

I often sat next to a lovely woman called Julie, who had obviously been told by Father Patrick to take me under her wing. It also explains why somewhat randomly she became my own godmother. My brother, sister and my dear friend Michelle were the others.

Church-related events figure quite rarely in my work now. Likewise one-to-ones with Hollywood film stars. But there was one unforgettable occasion, which came about because of my role as a judge in the annual *Observer/Guardian* Ethical Awards (which Nick finds very amusing, for some reason). There were quite a few of us: the journalist Lucy Siegle, TV star Ben Fogle, documentary presenter Stacey Dooley, wonderful 'Dragon' Deborah Meaden, and the ethical designer Livia

Giuggioli, who just happens to be married to the 'major Hollywood film star' Colin Firth.

I contained myself. There was no reason to assume he would attend every event his wife went along to, although on this occasion Nick came with me. It was all very glamorous. We had seats reserved in the front row so I could reach the stage easily, and Livia was a few seats along.

'Oh hello, Martine. How are you? Nice to meet you, Nick. My husband should be here in a minute.'

'*Colin?*' I blurted, before I could stop myself.

'Yeah, yeah. He's always late. Ha ha.'

I tried to make it look as though this conversation hadn't affected me like a high-powered cattle prod. I channelled sedate calm as I duly went up on stage to present the award. I did not fall over. Then, with a quiet fanfare in my brain, Colin did indeed arrive and sat about three places away, next to his wife. Obviously from that moment on my concentration was completely wrecked and I spent the rest of the ceremonials fidgeting and sliding around in my chair, trying to take an unobtrusive peek.

When the presentations were over, the usual chit-chat over drinks began. I tried, I really tried, not to do it but I had no choice. I went over to Liv and said, unashamedly, 'Look, I never do this. But I'd love to have photo taken with you and your husband.' She was great.

'Yes, no problem. Let's do it.'

'All right, brilliant. And don't worry, my husband's a photographer, so he'll be able to take it without a hitch.'

I'd already asked Nick if he wanted to be in it and, naturally, he'd rather have pulled out his own fingernails. He was quite happy to be behind the camera, which was, in fact, my phone. Liv rounded up her husband, who said hello. Through this big cheesy grin I said, 'Hi, I'm Martine. I apologise. I don't normally do this but I thought I had to take the opportunity.'

'No problem at all,' he said, politely.

Nick said, 'Look this way!'

'Quick, Nick. Got it? Yep. Lovely. Bye.'

I practically snatched the phone out of Nick's hand to see the work of art that I was going to send to all my mates. Oh God. He didn't have the flash on. You couldn't see a thing. I marry a bloody photographer and the only time I've ever wanted a photo with a famous person and he's buggered it up. To be fair, the situation was quite stressful. He was being hurried and having trouble turning the camera app on (probably something to do with me never updating my phone).

There was only one thing for it. They were still in the room. It was a once in a lifetime (well, *twice* in a lifetime, to be strictly accurate) chance. I had – HAD – to ask them again. I went up to them and said, more to Liv than Colin, 'I'm so sorry. My husband . . . well, he hasn't really taken the photo. It didn't come out very well.' I resisted the urge to say, 'He didn't put the bloody flash on.'

'Sure, no problem,' she said. 'Look, there's another guy with a camera. Let's get him over.'

Nick was demoted to onlooker and the photo was successfully taken. I still have it on my phone. Colin looks a bit like Mr Darcy at an unfashionable country ball, i.e. not thrilled, but as soon as we left that night I sent a million texts to my friends. 'Look who I've spent the evening with' the caption said, exultantly.

For one final flourish of name-dropping I should probably mention being lined up by Microsoft for an event at the Excel Arena – our Paralympic venue, by coincidence – where I was asked to speak to an audience of thousands, just before Steven Hawking. All in all, I thought I'd leave the theoretical physics to him.

Few people on earth know what Hollywood fame feels like. I'm definitely not one of them. I don't feel famous at all. I think I'm a normal person; a mum, daughter, sister, auntie, wife and friend. I don't love celebrity. I haven't got a huge ego. I'm really happy to balance the public things I do with a private life surrounded by family and my mates.

I do get recognised when I'm out in Tring, though. But that's pretty logical. As home towns go, it's pretty small, and I'm the only Paralympian with no legs living there. If someone asks, 'Are you Martine Wright?' I can't very well say no. Two missing legs is a bit of a giveaway.

I don't mind anyway. At my level of recognition, it's really nice to talk to people. It happens all the time in the local supermarket, but that's because I have a terrible habit of loading what I want in my lap and then wheeling round to find where Mum left the trolley. Quite often, if I take a bend a bit fast it all drops on the floor before I get there. Everyone down the aisle then stops what they're doing and helps me load up again.

It always makes me laugh, especially as it reminds me of the old *Crackerjack* cabbage game that I used to watch as a kid. 'Double or Drop' it was called, where each of three contestants had to answer questions. If they got one right they were given a toy to hold. If they got it wrong they were given a cabbage. If they dropped anything they were out. One day I reckon the checkout girl will say to me, 'Oooh, I could crush a grape'.

10

Roving in Rio

I'd like to say I'm the love of my husband's life. I am, however, well aware it's a very close-run thing – with *Star Wars*. Nick is the full-package fan. When the films first came out in the 1970s, he queued up for hours outside cinemas. He knows every character inside out. He can quote reams of dialogue. He actually does a very dodgy impersonation of the Evil Emperor with the hood of his fleece over his head. Naturally Oscar is now exactly the same.

'Who's that, then?' I sometimes say, pointing at the screen when I find him watching an episode for the umpteenth time. I'm going for a bit of mother-son bonding here. He just rolls his eyes.

'That's Anakin Skywalker,' he answers, in a tone somewhere between exasperation and pity.

This goes part way to explain the manic excitement in the Wiltshire/Wright household when I was summoned to a coffee shop in Berkhamsted to discuss *being in* Episode 7 of the *Star Wars* series – as a droid. This lovely chap, Pierre, is one of the senior prop directors, and he explained that the producers were looking for very fit amputees who would make excellent conversions into androids.

I'm sipping cappuccino, trying to keep a lid on my feelings.

'We're using CGI but we also want to include some real droids in it,' he said.

'Rii-ght,' I said slowly, brilliantly disguising the *Ohmygod, ohmygod, ohmygod* being played on a loop in my brain.

He whipped out his phone and showed me the designs they were imagining for the new androids. One looked a bit Daleky, like a big square box. The other had a more rounded top, as though it was wearing a helmet. I didn't care. I'd have worn a giant kettle to be in the film.

'How do you walk?' he asked.

I did a short demo around the café.

'Oh, your knees bend, don't they?' He didn't sound too happy about this.

'Don't worry, don't worry. They don't have to. I can walk on straight legs. I can go to my hospital and get a new set . . .' Anything, anything.

He pulled out a copy of what looked like *War and Peace*. It was the non-disclosure agreement because, back in

2013, the making of the new episode of *Star Wars* was absolutely huge news.

'We'll be in touch,' he said.

I was ready to go to Pinewood Studios there and then. My husband and son were beside themselves when I told them. Nick was little short of shellshocked, already imagining the première, sharing the red carpet with Harrison Ford, although I've no idea how he would have handled it in reality. But then, about three months later, we received the email: 'At the moment the droid for Martine is not required'. Heartbreak. I'm thinking how can a *Star Wars* film have *too many* droids? I don't mind being a bit part in a crowd scene. I'd have cancelled everything to do it. We didn't even discuss the fee. I'd have done it for nothing.

Martin, my agent, followed up from time to time. The last communication said: 'I'm sure it's only a matter of time before we need Martine's help'. So I live in hope.

After something like that you think there's no bolt from the blue that will ever take you by surprise again, but then I had another one. British Volleyball had decided not to send a team to Rio. They didn't have the funding to support it. I was now the proud captain of the team but I accepted the decision. It made sense to concentrate on small tournaments around the world to build up the confidence of the new players, rather than drop them in the deep end at a tournament they couldn't win. I could mourn the fact that maybe the London

Paralympics was a one-time wonder for me, but I couldn't change it. Then I had a phone call. How would I like to go to Rio to cover the 2016 Paralympics as a broadcaster for Channel 4? It wasn't a given. I'd have to pass an audition and do a great deal of training, but the option was there if I wanted it.

Once more I ran the film of conflicting responsibilities through my mind. One side: Oscar (who was nearly primary school age), Nick, family, home life, work versus the sporting carnival that would be Rio, plus caipirinhas. Actually, I'm retrospectively planting the thought of caipirinhas – the Brazilian national cocktail made mostly of sugarcane hard liquor – but even without the foreknowledge of those beauties it was a pretty enticing prospect.

I thought about it. I had, after all, covered the Invictus Games, the international sporting event for wounded, injured or sick men and women from the services that was the brainchild of Prince Harry. These games were a window on the world of phenomenal people who weren't famous like elite athletes but just as ferocious, determined and had that unflinching will to win. It was an honour to be asked, and I ended up commentating on them twice, specifically on the sitting volleyball with the BBC's lovely Jonathan Legard and Chris Mitchell. They could not have been more encouraging. Although, when someone like me has one of those face microphones attached to their chin, like Madonna in concert, they don't really need much encouragement.

I made my decision. I told Channel 4 yes. I'd give it ago.

This meant, first of all, a day-long interview and practice session with the TV presenter, Ian Blandford, whose company helps coach people to talk naturally in front of a camera. I turned up at this huge house in Clapham, south London, and was shown to the office at the bottom of his garden. He stuck a camera on me and asked me to talk about myself. I found it quite hard and reverted to speech-giving mode when he stopped me and said, 'No, no, you sound like you're giving a talk to about two thousand people. Television is different. You need to be personal and connect with people. Think of one individual, not a crowd.'

I wasn't sure how well I was doing but I'm quite old school about meetings and interviews. I'd done my research.

'Weren't you an electrician once?' I asked.

'How do you know that?' he said, surprised.

Maybe it was that bit of homework that swung it for me. I'd made the cut. The next stage of my TV training would take place at Princess Studios, above Bayswater shopping centre. This was going to be a three-day endurance test and some serious competition was attending.

I was very nervous turning up on the first morning. I recognised quite a few of the people there and many of them were experienced professionals, like the former Paralympic basketball player, Ade Adepitan; Iwan Thomas, who'd made me cry on the parade team bus back in 2012; the Paralympic swimming gold medalist Liz Johnson; former wheelchair rugby player Steve Brown; Lewis Hamilton's younger brother Nicolas ... the list went on. There were about ten of us in all. It was daunting.

Liz I knew already. She was one of our motivators down in Bath when the GB sitting volleyball team was getting ready for London. She basically had us all in tears, telling us the story of her mother being very ill and then dying while she was away at the Paralympics in Beijing. She had to make the decision then whether to fly back home or compete but knew what her mum, Bonnie, would have wanted. She swam her race and won the gold. 'I think it would make Mum happy,' she said.

When we were all gathered together it was explained that Channel 4 was looking for a whole mishmash of everything for their coverage, from presenters and reporters to individual sports specialists and pundits.

The first thing we had to do was sit on the TV sofa and introduce ourselves. 'Tell us something we don't know about you and what you're looking forward to from today' was the only instruction. When it was my turn, I settled on the coach and said, 'Hello, my name's Martine Wright and my most random job in the past was being a milkwoman. I'm looking forward to learning new things and hopefully getting a job from it.'

That was my first mistake. Everyone else, when we played them back, said uplifting things about looking forward to witnessing wonderful sport first-hand, inspiring the national team, meeting new people and so on, and I virtually said, 'All I want is a job'. I sighed inwardly. That's gone down badly, I thought. I suppose you could argue I was honest.

Next was scripts and autocue. This made me nervous too. I'd never done autocue before, and the script wasn't made up of the kind of words I'd naturally use. On top of that I was no wide-ranging sports expert either. The subject was heavily geared towards athletics and swimming. Not my area of expertise, which was pretty much . . . sitting volleyball. I'd had to do huge amounts of research to prepare myself, but I was still feeling desperately unsure of myself. I also had a tendency to say 'blind' when I should be saying 'visually impaired'.

We were doing a mock-up of a sofa presentation. I was paired with the former marine commander, JJ Chambers, who was also new to this kind of thing. I tried to relax, although I was having trouble with the earpiece. I lost thirty per cent of my hearing from the 7/7 explosion, so catching the fuzzy words in my ear was proving challenging. But I could make out the instruction: 'Now go to the break, teeing up the athletes we'll be looking at next'. OK, I could do that.

The autocue was primed with their names. I saw that Natalie Du Toit, the formidable Paralympic swimmer who'd won thirteen gold medals between Athens, Beijing and London, was coming up. She's about as well-known as it gets; one of only three Paralympians ever to also compete in the Olympics.

'JJ,' I hissed. 'How do you pronounce her name?'

'Toit,' he said promptly. 'As in "hoity-toity".'

Yep, got that. Toit, Toit, Toit, I repeated silently, to get it completely stuck in my brain. I daren't get that wrong. Then I took a deep breath and embarked on my announcement.

'And coming back after the break we have Hannah Cockroft in the two-hundred metres, GB star Jonnie Peacock, and then a special feature on the brilliant South African swimmer, Natalie Du . . . Twat.'

Don't ask me how I said that when I knew full well it was Toit. To make it worse I then burst out laughing. This was supposed to be a professional, as-if-live performance. Instead I was sitting there, roaring with laughter, my head in my hands, while the voices in my ear were barking furiously: 'Apologise now, apologise now, quickly.'

I couldn't say anything at all. I just lost it, still laughing. JJ looked bewildered, wondering what the hell to do to recover. To be fair, everyone in the studio had cracked up too and all I could eventually do was keep repeating: 'I'm sorry, I'm sorry, I'm sorry,' with a big grin on my face. I'm told this moment has been immortalised by media trainers everywhere as a classic demonstration of What Not To Do.

My self-confidence had taken another huge hit. I was sure they'd cross my name off the list now. I tried to compensate by doing what seemed like hundreds of hours of research on disability sport from all over the world. But as fast as I fed it into my memory, it seemed to leak out again.

By the final day of the three, I noticed a couple of people had not reappeared. Presumably they hadn't made the cut. It encouraged me slightly that I was still there. A number of executive producers arrived to watch us, including Michael Cole, which added to my nerves. I found myself offering him cups of coffee – 'One lump or two?' – as my contribution to proceedings. Everyone was talking about the athletics in Doha. I realised, with a pang, I knew bugger all about the athletics in Doha. When we finally broke up and went home I had no idea whether I'd be going to Rio or not. Nothing was said. Was that bad news or not?

One month later the call came. I was being offered a job as 'roving reporter' at the 2016 Paralympic Games. Initially I felt deflated. I thought I'd be one for the sofa. This was Natalie Du Toit coming back to haunt me. But I revised my thinking almost immediately. I was going to Rio with Channel 4. This was amazing. What an opportunity! I was so lucky. How could I possibly say no, even though I discovered – looking at the dates of travel in September – that I'd be walking out of the door to go to Brazil on the very day that Oscar would be going to his first day at primary school. Sod's law.

For the next three months I was rehearsing in studios,

mugging up on athletics and getting more and more nervous. Now this was getting real. I don't think, even including the 2012 Paralympics, I'd ever been more stressed. The more revision I did, the more nervous I became. I was petrified I'd be asked live on air something I couldn't answer.

I kept saying to Martin, my agent: 'Find out what sports I'm doing.'

He kept coming back: 'They don't know yet.'

About a month before we were due to fly to Rio I was driving to a speaking job in Bristol and working myself up to a real attack of anxiety. I hadn't been sleeping. Nick knew I was upset and had been trying to calm me down but nothing was working. My friend Alex had called me earlier and I was due to call her back. I rang her on my hands-free from the M4. She'd barely said hello when I burst into sobs, crying hysterically at the same time as trying to speak.

'Martine, what's wrong? I can't understand you.'

More sobbing.

'Pull over, we can talk,' she said. So I pulled off the motorway at the next junction and she calmed me down.

'Don't worry,' she said. 'Break it down, like we used to do in sales. If someone asks you a question you don't know, start talking generally and then focus on something you *do* know. Or throw back a question. You'll be fine. They haven't given you the job because you're a sports expert. They've given it to you because you're you.'

I was gulping and hiccupping by now, a sign that the storm was subsiding. It helped talking to such a good mate and part of me suspected she was right. They couldn't possibly have mistaken me for a talking encyclopedia, so maybe they had spotted something else. It's funny how we torture ourselves with all the things we're not. I didn't have legs any more. That didn't stop me. Maybe I should learn from my own example.

The next big event was the launch of the Channel 4 coverage and the unveiling of the presenters. This was a major, glitzy, red-carpet affair and I was sitting next to legends like Clare Balding and Frank Gardner, the BBC security correspondent who was partially paralysed having been shot six times while working in Saudi Arabia in 2004. Sportspeople such as the wheelchair athlete Hannah Cockroft were there, and Sophie Christiansen, who had found out only that day that she and her horse Athene had qualified for Rio in the Paralympic dressage. She went on to win three more golds in Brazil and was one of the huge stars of 2016 *SPOTY*.

I thought, Blimey, I am in seriously exalted company here. It might have rattled me but then lovely Clare Balding came over and gave me a big hug. It made me feel as though I belonged. It's yet another thing on the list of the qualities that make her so great to be around.

I had a job the next morning, so there was no question of it being an all-night party for me. I left quite early and bumped into Phil Spencer, as in Kirsty and Phil from

Location, Location, Location – the house-hunting programme in which Nick and I had once 'starred'.

'Hey, Phil!' I called, never one to leave a chit-chat
unexploited.

'Martine!' he yelled back. 'What are you doing here?'

We caught up on our news, took a selfie, and I made
him promise to give Kirsty my love. It reminded me of
traumas/laughs we had on the programme, searching
for a wheelchair-friendly bungalow when Nick and I
wanted to move on from our house-with-the-lift in
Berkhamsted.

It was just before our wedding when life was understandably busy. I'd recently been in hospital, where Hasu
had done an operation on my arm, regrafting the skin so
I was wedding-dress ready. We'd applied to the programme months before and heard nothing. I'd forgotten
all about it. But as I regained consciousness following the
operation, completely woozy from the general anaes-
thetic, I had a vision of Nick in front of my face saying,
'Babe! Babe! Kirsty and Phil! Kirsty and Phil have called!'
Only it wasn't a vision. It was real. *Location, Location,
Location* was going to help us find a bungalow.

Two months later we were filming. Unfortunately for
Nick the first day of the shoot was immediately after his
stag weekend. He'd come back on the Sunday night in
absolute bits and, on Monday morning, 'bright' and early,
we had to be at the SnowDome in Milton Keynes for
heart-to-heart interviews on camera. I sat on a mono-ski,

talking, while Nick stood behind me looking rough and swaying slightly.

After a few false starts we eventually found the home we live in now, in Tring. Although, when we found rampant woodworm under the floorboards I thought I'd keep a bit of it and show it to Phil as a joke next time I saw him. Meeting Kirsty Allsopp was great. The first time I met her she said, 'Did you know my uncle was an amputee? It didn't stop him doing anything.'

His injury had been caused by a bomb, which was a coincidence. But it was an unexploded bomb, which fell on him and crushed one of his legs.

I've only bumped into her once since the show, at an International Women's Day gathering at 10 Downing Street. We'd both had baby Oscars at about the same time, so there was plenty to talk about and I was very chuffed already about meeting Rita and Mavis out of *Coronation Street*.

Seeing Phil at Channel 4 that night was a sudden reminder of all the crazy things that just seemed to go on happening. And now Rio. On one side, stress; on the other, huge excitement. Between the launch and the flight to Brazil another phone call came in. Did I fancy writing a column for *The Times* during the Paralympics? And they didn't mean the *Edgware & Mill Hill Times*. This was an extraordinary request. *The Times*. One of the most famous and respected newspapers in the world. I said I would if they helped me with the writing, because I knew that between research, reporting and sleeping there would scarcely be a spare minute for seventeen days.

I must have been psychic. My prediction proved to be completely right.

There was only a few days to go before my flight, and I was still asking, desperately, which sports I'd be assigned when word finally came: table tennis and archery. I felt, if I'm honest, the deep clang of let-down. The last time I played table tennis was at St Andrew's Church youth club in Edgware, when I was about ten. It didn't thrill me then, let alone now. And archery was a sport I found pretty annoying when I tried it at that Paralympic taster day.

I had a brainwave. I called up one of the Channel 4 producers I knew and told him I used to play wheelchair tennis and that I knew a few of the players.

'I'm sure I'll be able to set up some great interviews and one-to-ones with the families as well,' I told him.

He went off to discuss it and came back with better news. 'OK, you're doing table tennis and tennis.'

Clearly I was going to have to mug up on table tennis. There was no escaping that. I'd only ever heard of our best player, Will Bayley, and was still convinced it was the most boring sport ever.

How utterly wrong can you be?

Rio was extraordinary and I'm now, undoubtedly, the number one fan of Paralympic table tennis. That story would unfold over ten days in a glorified hanger near the

Broadcast Centre where the competition was held. But first I was being catapulted into a hot seat for the opening ceremony, as part of the live coverage alongside Clare Balding and *The Last Leg*'s brilliant host, Adam Hills. For the first time in living memory I was wearing *a skirt*. This was Jane's doing, the stylist, who asked me if I ever wore dresses. Absolutely not, I said. I'd only worn a dress once and that was on my wedding day. 'How about a jeans skirt?' she persisted.

'No,' I said firmly. 'No, no, no.'

I went on air with a jeans skirt on. Loved it. I wear it all the time now. And dresses. Sometimes you just have to get over yourself. Anyway, the skirt wasn't the issue during the opening ceremony. It was the lack of an earpiece. Clare was asking me things about the dazzling scene below in the Maracanã Stadium and I could hardly hear a word she said. The noise, ramped up by fireworks, music, bands and 80,000 people going mad was indescribable.

There was a beautiful moment when Brazil's greatest ever Paralympic swimmer, Clodoaldo Silva, navigated his wheelchair up a flight of steps to light the Olympic cauldron, demonstrating, truly, that 'Nothing Is Impossible'. But I was beginning to doubt that slogan by the end of our broadcast, when the whole place was going carnival crazy and I was straining to hear a single word. I was leaning forward, trying to catch the drift, my face wrinkled in deep concentration. I do hope nobody was watching. Luckily this was about 3 a.m. back in Britain, so I reckoned most people I knew would have long gone to bed. No one's ever mentioned it.

The next day my TV reporting career began in earnest. For some, Rio may have been one long riot of colour, noise, sport, drama, restaurants, beaches, cocktails and fun, fun, fun. In my case 'carnival' Rio was something I glimpsed fleetingly en route between my hotel room and the two tennises I'd been sent to cover. I can't say I was entirely relaxed. I was armed with the Channel 4 Paralympic bible, which contained huge amounts of info on the athletes, and I was doing my own online research. I was trawling the *British Paralympic Association Handbook* but I still wasn't sure I knew my two assigned sports inside out.

Then I made a key discovery. Never mind the statistics, talk to a human. Especially one called Fran, who was the media liaison officer for the table tennis in Rio.

'Martine!' she exclaimed, adding reasonably, 'What are you doing here?' When I told her she said, 'Don't worry. I've got everything you need.'

Fran had looked after me and the sitting volleyball team during the London Paralympics. My shaky ground had suddenly become a whole lot more solid. She briefed me every day, helping me speak to the athletes and get to know their families.

That worked for me. I may have been holding the microphone but, because I was a Paralympian myself only four years previously, I completely understood their motivations and disappointments – almost to the point where I wanted to forget the questions and give them a cuddle. This may not be entirely professional but it produced, I'm told, one of the best interviews of the entire Paralympics.

I'd basically bonded with GB's superstar showman table tennis player Will Bayley. His mum, Chrissie, was probably the most enthusiastic parent in Brazil, yelling, 'COME ON, WILL!' at full volume, non-stop, through all his matches. It clearly worked because he won his way through to the final against the Brazilian favourite, Israel Stroh, and I had a terrible feeling I was going to get as worked up as his mum.

He was desperately trying to overcome the haunting memory of his silver medal at the London Paralympics, when he lost to a guy he'd beaten eight times in their nine previous matches. He'd collapsed in tears when he lost, and one of the unforgettable images of the 2012 Games was him being comforted by his conquering opponent. I could completely understand why his heart and soul were on the line in the upcoming match.

He'd overcome cancer at the age of seven and had endured a lifelong congenital muscle-wasting disease that had attacked all four of his limbs. It affected his joints, legs, fingers and toes. He'd needed dozens of operations throughout his life to help correct the ravages of his condition. He'd been heartbroken in London and it had taken him years to get over it. He took himself, alone, to China to train with the greatest table tennis regime on earth to improve his play, mentally as much as physically. He was emotional, passionate, funny and massively determined.

'When I first came into the team, GB were laughed off the table,' he told the media. 'The Chinese, Ukrainians, thought we were muppets.'

He'd been key in changing all that.

I sat up close and courtside for the match. It was proper nail-biting stuff. I could hear him muttering things under his breath. More 'COME ON, WILL' from his mum. ('She's mental, like me,' he'd once told me, affectionately.) There was no question of me being an unbiased reporter. I was cheering like a banshee. After making the winning shot, in pure exultation, he leapt onto the table with his hands in the air, taking the acclaim. This was against the rules, so the referee held up a yellow card. He just jumped down and gave the woman a huge hug. I'd love to see that catch on in football. No more effing and jeffing at the ref; just give him a sweaty cuddle.

Moments later he was standing in front of me, sweaty, proud and deliriously happy, draped in a union flag. I went through the usual questions for a post-gold-medal interview live on air: 'How does it feel?' and the rest. But then a little nudging thought came into my head – I remembered the story of his nan.

'When you were seven years old and your grandma bought you that table tennis table, did you ever imagine you would be Paralympic champion?'

That opened the floodgates. He tried to talk while crying buckets at the same time. I abandoned journalistic distance and went for the full hug instead, appearing in vision on the nation's TV screens to give him a massive cuddle. You're not supposed to do that, but I couldn't help myself. I suspected I might be in trouble. Instead, the feedback was that they loved it. Back during the London 2012 celebrations, Iwan Thomas confessed that making me cry on TV had earned him extra brownie points. Now I'd earned my own. But I was just genuinely thrilled for Will, totally caught up in the moment. It was my highlight of the Games.

By then I'd bonded with the whole table tennis team, to be honest, and cuddled pretty much every player whether they liked it or not. We had a right laugh as well. I was hopeless at journalistic detachment. I seemed to be living every shot. When Aaron McKibbin, Ross Wilson and Will won a team bronze later in the tournament, I was so happy I ended up kissing them all. It only struck me afterwards that this was possibly inappropriate for a woman old enough to be their mum. But sometimes you've just got to celebrate.

I blame the atmosphere. It whips you up into a mad world where nothing matters except the next point of a match and where people who were strangers to you a week ago suddenly assumed the status of beloved friends.

Every night I'd get back to my hotel room shattered. I had an oven and a dishwasher in my room but I was always too tired and too late to cook. Tearing open a crisp packet felt beyond me some evenings. In fact, my greatest discovery was bumping into Alex Brooker, another of *The Last Leg* presenters, in the lift, clutching a Domino's pizza.

'Oh God, where d'you get that?' I demanded. He said reception had sorted it out. It's hard to describe the simple joy this news brought me.

There was no time for fine dining. Work was full on. I'd meet Clare Balding very early over breakfast sometimes and she'd give me an encouraging pep talk. I think I'm pretty energetic but she obviously runs on everlasting batteries. By the time I was given one afternoon off, as a reward for the Will Bayley interview, I was very ready for it. Keith the cameraman and Andy the soundman were obviously allowed a break too, and we headed for the beach together. Copacabana was too far, so we staggered to a nearby beach bar and spent a wonderful afternoon drinking beer and admiring the view, which largely consisted of bodybuilders and silicone-enhanced beach volleyball bums.

I was wafted away temporarily to a world of delicious *frutos do mar*, a spectacular sunset and beautiful relaxation. Then wafted back again on a trip to the loo when I met the most lovely family from Sunderland who had saved hard to come and support their 19-year-old son, the British Para swimmer, Matt Wylie. They summed up the spirit of the Paralympics for me: stopping at nothing to travel halfway round the world, somehow finding accommodation and the price of a ticket for those few moments in the swimming pool when their son would contest an event with as much chance of failure as success. At this precise moment, they were stuck. They couldn't find a taxi anywhere, so we gave them a lift in our Channel 4 minibus and wished them all the luck in the world. Our wish came true. Matt won gold in the fifty metres freestyle.

As things wound down at the table tennis hanger, the rules were bending slightly. For a while I'd been in trouble for constantly zipping into non-journalistic areas to grab a word with Fran. Some of the officials turned a blind eye, like a friendly Brazilian guy called Bruno. But poor Bruno was getting it in the neck from his boss, who regarded my incursions as an outrage. I carried on anyway.

I suppose one enemy out of thousands was a small price to pay. Then I bumped into her at the very end of the competition. There was a match on one of the tables but no were Brits involved, so I didn't have to pay attention, but I thought I might be in for some aggravation.

'Oh, hi,' she said, 'can I make you a cup of tea?' Obviously my incursions on the wrong side of a piece of rope were all forgotten now. We started chatting.

'Do you live here in Brazil?' I asked, making polite conversation.

'No, I live in China actually.'

'Oh, China. I've got a mate who's lived over there for

years. Obviously you won't know her amongst one-point-three billion. Where do you live?'

'Shanghai.'

'Ha, that's funny. Sarah's in Shanghai. She's just moved back.'

'What's her name?'

'Sarah Jones.'

'You are having a laugh?'

'No, you don't know her, do you?'

'She's one of my mates. We share the same tattoo artist.'

By now we are actually screaming at one another in shock. What an incredible coincidence. In fact, we were so loud, someone was sent from the judging panel to tell us to keep the noise down. It was a fittingly crazy end to a fantastic tournament.

The British Paralympic wheelchair tennis brought home another haul of medals – bronze, silver and one gold for Gordon Reid in the men's singles when he overcame fellow Brit, Alfie Hewett. The women's team didn't do quite as well as expected, perhaps due to Jordanne Whiley's wrist injury, but she and teammate Lucy Shuker still managed bronze in the doubles. Watching the action took me back eight years. Wheelchair tennis had been my chosen sport until I discovered I was pregnant with Oscar. Maybe it could have been me out there in the Rio sunshine. Sliding doors . . . but I knew I had no regrets. I loved the team element of sitting volleyball and, to prove the point, I was utterly thrilled to see my old teammate

Emma Wiggs storming to victory and her first Paralympic gold in the K1 rowing final. Wiggsy had finally achieved her personal dream.

I was in make-up as the race was being shown live on TV. As fast as Sherree, the make-up artist, was applying my mascara, I was weeping it off. 'That's my mate!' I was hiccupping in explanation. I was absolutely thrilled for her. It couldn't have happened to a more dedicated, determined and gutsy athlete who had tried so hard to bring the same qualities to our rather-less-than-mean machine sitting volleyball team during the previous Paralympics. This was her reward. And I was so happy for her.

Beyond the sport, I still had one other duty to perform: presents for the family back home. But between working, working and working, I'd had no time to go shopping. I was staying in a complex near the Broadcast Centre, and apart from a supermarket there were no retail outlets at all. What was I supposed to buy them, a pound of potatoes and a pineapple? It was all becoming a bit of a trauma.

As so often happens, something turned up. I met a friendly woman in the Channel 4 edit suite.

'Oh, they're nice flip-flops,' I said, noticing the colourful Havaianas she was wearing.

'There's a little kiosk round the corner selling them,' she replied.

The solution to my dilemma. I explained the situation.

'I'll get you some,' she offered.

'No, no, it'll be too much trouble.' I was totting up the numbers I'd need to buy.

She insisted.

'OK, I need fifteen pairs,' I said, writing down all the names.

She looked at it. 'What about you?' she asked.

I was wearing long jeans and trainers at the time. I lifted up my trouser leg with a grin.

'God, I'm so sorry.'

'Don't worry,' I laughed and reassured her. 'It's just that my flip-flop-wearing days are probably over.'

My last night in Brazil was the closing ceremony followed by a knees-up at the British House, the building the BPA had commandeered for the athletes to use as their second home throughout the Games. This was my moment to try the famous caipirinha cocktails I'd heard so much about but never had time to sample. I can report they were excellent, and served with a dangerous frequency. The celebration was immense. GB finished second in the medal table and it was hard to argue with the feeling that these were the greatest Paralympic Games, from the British perspective, that we had ever seen. London will always be the most special to me, as it was the one where I'd actually competed, but to be ringside in Rio was a stupendous privilege that I will never forget.

I did forget, however, much of that last night, owing to the onslaught of alcohol. Bedtime was somewhere around

4 a.m. and then I had to catch the plane home to London. Exhausted athletes were scattered throughout the cabin, yearning to go to sleep or watch a film, but the British Airways crew were so excited to have them on board they kept interrupting with announcements. 'Right, everybody up. We're going to sing the national anthem now!'

You could see some of the swimmers – they're renowned party animals – sinking lower and lower in their seats with their headphones on, desperately hoping no one noticed them. Their body language was screaming: 'Shut up. Leave me alone. I'm knackered.'

The swimmer sitting next to me, unluckily for him, was clearly in possession of a gold medal. I eyed it hungrily.

'I don't suppose,' I asked cheekily, 'you'd let me put that round my neck, would you, for a picture?'

What could the poor bloke say?

'I don't usually do that,' he grumbled reluctantly, 'but all right. Go on then.'

I still have the picture on my iphone. Thank you, Sascha Kindred. He has seven Paralympic gold medals, so I'm amazed he couldn't spare one . . .

I remember the homecoming vividly. As soon as I landed at Heathrow I had to call CNN because I was doing an appearance for them the next day. It was 10 a.m. as I groggily dialled the number.

'Oh, hello, Martine. We're really looking forward to seeing you later.'

'What d'you mean *later*? It's tomorrow.'

'No, it's later today. Everyone's very excited.'

I made a second phone call, this time in tears to my husband at work.

'I'm completely shattered, and I've got to be in Woking . . .'

He listened patiently. I bet he was thinking, Yep, Martine's home.

11

The Power of 7

O n 7 July 2005 I was just a woman going to work. I had a hangover, but there wasn't much else wrong with my world. My job was fun, jetting around the world as an international marketing manager on a good salary. I was energetic, ambitious and particularly excited that morning, as the Olympics were coming to London, my turf, my home city. I'd run up the escalator in my new trainers, despite the effect of the previous night's celebrations. And there was a train just pulling into Moorgate station. What a result! I jumped on, grabbed my favourite seat, and started reading my newspaper.

Olympics. Olympics. Wall-to-wall Olympics. I'm turning the pages and promising myself I'll find a way to get tickets. I don't look up at all, totally preoccupied. I don't see a man with a rucksack. I have no idea he is about to detonate a bomb to kill and maim as many innocent people as possible in the morning rush hour. And in the split second it takes for him to commit suicide and murder seven people I'm not that version of Martine Wright any more.

Twelve years on, I'm still optimistic, positive, up for a laugh, loving, sociable, a bit of a control freak. But the trauma and its aftermath changed me. Corporate life wasn't as important any more. Worrying about the little stuff didn't matter. Making five-year, ten-year plans, why on earth would you bother? The important things were right there alongside me all the time. Being close to family, seeing old friends, making new ones. Sport for the endorphins and the bonding; cold Stella for the parties and laughs. It's all quite simple really.

I think I knew these things deep down even before I leapt on that train. I'd been fantasising about giving up my job and opening a café in London somewhere. Not a flash 'I'll have a latte' café, but a greasy spoon where builders would come in with their boots and their wise-cracks and I'd fry the eggs and give as good as I got.

I hadn't done anything about it. I'm not sure I would have done. Then fate gave me no option. Don't get me wrong. When I say I know what's important and what to let go these days, it doesn't mean I always follow my own advice. I can still get incredibly upset about trivial things – missed planes, lost phones, tyres blowing out on the motorway. I'm not serene. I'm definitely not the Dalai Lama.

What I am is happy. It's an irony that such a hugely, hugely negative event has given me a life and career that I love in every single respect. Except possibly the unbridled chaos of my schedule. Who wouldn't love standing up in front of people, talking? Well, my husband, wouldn't; he'd be appalled. But for me, it's the greatest occupation in the world. I soon realised I didn't miss sitting behind a desk, tapping at a keyboard, un-jamming paper from a printer.

It turns out you don't need legs to do the things I do. I have gone so far beyond anything I'd once imagined for myself. Flying a plane, jumping out of one, *competing for my country at the Paralympics*. I've entered a new life beyond my wildest dreams while still being fortunate enough to do the traditional things like getting married, having babies, buying a home.

I look back and I see a string of events and adventures that have brought me great, often unexpected, joy. An absolute highlight was appearing in a one-off BBC *Strictly* special for *Sport Relief* with the six-foot-four gorgeousness of professional dancer Ian Waite. To dance again, even in a wheelchair, was a very poignant thing, especially with my family in the audience. It reminded me that Dad's seventieth birthday party was one of the very first outings I'd made after leaving hospital in 2005. He loves his dancing, so we promised each other that we'd dance together that night. It was a big thing for me just a year after losing my legs. But we did it. Dad cried and all his guests cheered.

No wonder I permanently have this sense that I'm lucky. I don't mean it's at the forefront of my mind every day but it's always there as an undercurrent. I don't think my family shares that feeling, after all the pain they've been through, and I definitely didn't think that myself during the first two years of my rehabilitation when the sight of a pair of my old Birkenstocks could hit me with a sense of terrible loss.

It would be mad to claim this contentedness happened at once. It didn't. It's been a process. I did worry that my 'disability', for want of a better word, would have an impact on me. I definitely had a massive worry about Oscar. Not being able to kick a ball around with him was the least of it. I remember a date night with Nick at a trendy restaurant when I spoiled the romance of the occasion by bursting into floods of tears over the prospect of other kids being cruel to Oscar because his mum was in a wheelchair.

It might still be a worry when he's older at secondary school but, for the time being, he comes home and says things like, 'Mrs Ing was speaking about you in school today, Mummy. She said that even when you lost your legs you didn't give up. She said we should try hard and do our best like you.'

Sometimes small difficulties hold me back. If I'm on holiday in Spain I give up on the idea of going in the sea, given the vast quantities of sand I'm going to get in unacceptable areas of my swimsuit. So I just accept it. It's actually quite nice sitting outside a restaurant with a small beer and tapas watching Nick and Oscar playing on the beach. It doesn't affect me being a mum. Oscar still calls out for me in the middle of the night when he's had a bad dream. You don't need legs to see off the bogeyman.

There are still times when I put my clothes on for a party and sigh momentarily with regret that I'm not all dolled up in a fabulous outfit and Louboutin high heels. It's usually jeans and Converse in my case. I think, what's the point of putting on make-up when it slides off again after thirty minutes of dancing? Wearing legs takes massive effort. I was told when I first learned to walk on those horrible rockers that it's 280 per cent harder for a double amputee above the knee to walk with prosthetic legs than normal ones. I think it's more. That figure may compute the physical exertion but can't possibly take into account the mental effort of being totally switched on all the time. Don't bother looking for a banana skin, just about everything in the outside world is a hazard. Wet ground, uneven ground, moss, a camber in the road; anything can literally trip you up. And it's hot work. Half my body is covered in silicon liners even before I put my legs on. That's like wearing a wetsuit to the party. Try dancing in one of those sometime and, because I now have half a body, there's less surface area to lose the heat.

My friends are great. They say I was always likely to fall over anyway, even when I did have legs. They point out I always was a 'sweaty cow'. That's why I love them so much. But I do worry about the day when I enter the menopause. I might be the first woman to react to hot flushes by actually spontaneously combusting. All human trace vanished except for a singed mark on a chair.

Overall I consider myself a very fortunate woman. I had my 'woe is me!' time in hospital when I couldn't get beyond the sight of my legs – or what was left of them. I took all that love and care from my family for granted. It was just a given. It fills me with wonder that Mum and Dad were there, twelve, fourteen, sometimes sixteen hours a day. Dashing down to the kitchen to find me toast or cereal for breakfast. Blagging an extra TV so I could watch *EastEnders* while Dad watched something else. First thing in the morning, last thing at night, they were there. Nick was doing a London bus tour every night just to be at my side. I knew nothing about arriving in hospital as 'Hotel Unknown' with life-threatening injuries, a blackened face and a body minus legs swollen to twice its normal size, but they had to see that. I don't remember being in a coma, hovering between life and death. Or being in intensive care. But they do. I didn't have to look in the mirror and see myself shrink down to six stone with a hospital bug, but they had to witness that.

Yet they wrapped me in a cocoon of strength and optimism. I have no doubt the care of my whole family and my friends kick-started my recovery. It was as important to me as the amazing treatment I received from the NHS.

It still upsets me when I think of all they must have suffered. That's why I'm constantly trying to do things now
that say: 'It's all right now. Life is good.' And it's why the
Paralympics and loads of other things I've done have
meant so much to me.

Perhaps it helped me that I never, ever, felt anger
towards the bombers or what happened to me. I simply
couldn't understand it. I know some of the other victims
felt huge personal anger towards the terrorists. It didn't
seem to arise in me. Perhaps I unconsciously asked myself,
Will it do me any good to feel angry? Is it going to help
me? No, it's not. So I won't. I understood the whole thing
was too big for me to comprehend. I let it go.

Fifty-two people died that day and I was still here. How
could I consider myself anything but lucky to still be
alive? Every one of those lost souls has given me a
strength to carry on, knowing it could have quite easily
been me. Over the years, I have felt guilty about thinking
this way as it might seem terribly selfish.

As time goes by I'm able to piece together specific
things that happened a little better, but it's not something
I want to dwell on. I now know the name of the bomber
on the Aldgate train. I can acknowledge the event as a
'bombing', as opposed to an 'accident', which I needed to
do for my sanity in the early years. But I don't rake over it
or live in the past.

When I got married, the *News of the World* asked me if
they could run photos of the bombed-out carriage and a

mugshot of the bomber alongside their feature. I understood they wanted to heighten the drama on their pages but at that stage I couldn't bear to see them. I said no. I couldn't even watch an episode of *EastEnders* where some of the cast were shown getting on a tube. I had to walk out of the room. I wasn't ready.

There were things, curiously small things in some cases, that took me years to get over. One was a looking inside a bag. I'd often carry a trendy embroidered leather bag to work with a change of shoes and other bits and pieces inside. I didn't have it with me the morning of 7/7, but I had taken it in the day before and it was still at the office. Eventually it found its way back to me. Kathy, my former boss, sent it back when it was clear I wouldn't be able to return to work after all. I couldn't look at it. I stashed it in a cupboard at our old house and it was only when we moved to Tring and it came to light again that I felt able to open it up. Inside I found a pair of old-school brown trainers and one more item that made me gasp. A newspaper. Dated 6 July 2005. A complete record of the day before the life I was living ended.

Similarly, one day about six months ago, Mum came round and said, 'I've got something for you.' She handed me a silver ring and bangle. I recognised them immediately. I'd been wearing them on the day. They'd been long gone. The police had taken them, perhaps used them in their forensic inquiries, I don't know, but they had eventually been returned to Mum in a plastic bag, still completely blackened from the smoke, and she'd been holding onto them until she thought I could handle seeing them again. Typically she'd polished them to a sparkling shine. 'I found them in a drawer,' she said casually when she gave them to me. Did she ever.

I often wear that bangle now. People think I'm mad. 'That's a nice bangle,' they say. 'Funnily enough I got blown up with it on,' is rarely the answer they're expecting. I suppose it's living proof that I'm strong enough now.

Grant said something to me in hospital very early on.

'Martine, out of the three of us – you, me and Tracey – I really don't know if me and Tracey could have handled this.'

I told him – and I still believe – that no one knows how they'll react in a crisis. It's a mystery that mercifully not everyone has to solve. But being a glass-half-full person definitely helped me, and maybe my brother saw that in me. I'll never forget a bracelet he gave me as a present engraved with the words: 'You Can Still Have Your Dreams'.

I suppose I deal with my turbulent emotions by expressing them and then expelling the bad stuff. I didn't realise it, but my body was doing the same thing. Amongst all my many injuries, I didn't even bother to mention a bump on my head under the hairline. I ignored it while I was in hospital. All kind of weird things were going on anyway. My hair was coming out in clumps and my nails had developed weird ridges across them horizontally. The doctors said my body was just being clever and not wasting its time with trivial stuff.

About eighteen months later this bump was getting bigger and bigger and eventually a full inch-long piece of metal shrapnel revealed itself. It had been there all along, and now it had come to the surface to be extracted. As they froze my scalp and whipped it out, it struck me as the perfect physical example of the way I'd tried to get rid of the trauma emotionally.

Even so, however resilient I've become, whenever 'breaking news' interrupts a TV or radio broadcast I get a sick lurch in the pit of my stomach, fearing it'll be announcing another terrible terrorist atrocity somewhere in the world. It's just a gut reaction. The truck attack in Nice on Bastille Day 2016 that killed eighty-four; the Christmas market attack in Berlin the same year, leaving twelve dead and over fifty injured; the shooting dead of thirty-eight people by a gunman at a holiday hotel in Tunisia in 2015 . . . they horrify me.

But it was the attack on Westminster in March 2017 that affected me most personally. I was numb initially. How do you compute the mind of a man who uses a car to mow down innocent people just strolling over Westminster Bridge, and then stabs to death a policeman on duty at the gates of the House of Parliament? The news kept repeating that it was the worst terrorist attack in London since the 7/7 bombings and as I watched the television, I thought this is what everyone must have gone through eleven years ago. Who do I call? Is everyone I love safe? Why haven't I heard from my friend, wife, husband, brother, sister, daughter, son? And I worried about Oscar, his generation and the one after that, ever onwards if these attacks go on and on, evolving and murdering, because they are so incredibly difficult to stop.

I wondered if the emergency information line worked better than it did for my poor parents, post 7/7, and then my thoughts flew to Liz Kenworthy who I knew had worked as a police officer at those very same Parliament gates for the last seven years. She would have known the officer who died. What an incredible, and sad, coincidence for her. She wasn't there on the day. She'd retired nine months beforehand . . . on 7 July 2016. She'd deliberately chosen that day to have a happier association with the date in her mind. I understood that completely.

After the Westminster attack I felt a desperate sorrow for the victims, just blameless people going about their normal lives. I always do with each fresh horror. But I must admit my first reaction is often with the families. The ones left behind. Their world has just been turned upside down. When I read that one woman had lost her son, brother and father in the Tunisian shootings I immediately thought how unbearably awful for her. It's not for me to put myself in her place but my heart went out to her.

Obviously, tragically, we live in a world where such

things will happen again and again. War and violence in all its different guises has been going on forever. As kids, my mum and dad used to shelter in the London underground during the Second World War. They'd hear the siren, grab a gas mask and run for cover. Unfortunately, given the nature of terrorism, you don't have a siren any more. No one's naive enough to think these atrocities are not going to keep happening. It's a cat and mouse game for the security services to catch the terrorists before they put their plots into action.

At least the horror of an atrocity is often matched by the selfless and heroic behaviour of the people around it. It's important to remember the good within the bad. When a German bomb fell through the roof onto Mum's living room couch during the Blitz, when she was a baby, a neighbour took in the whole family. And I sometimes wonder whether the 7/7 bombers decided to cause their deadly havoc on that day because London had been so alive with joy and celebration the day before. It was a deliberate act to sabotage the good.

I have no answers to the issue of terrorism today. I just wish that young people who feel that strapping a bomb to their chest and blowing themselves up is a gateway to a better life could be persuaded otherwise. And that all of us could be a bit more aware of one another – the dangers and the kindnesses. Imagine a London where people looked out for each other instead of focusing on their papers or phones all the time. Just as it was during London

2012, when we all actually spoke to one another. That was a wonderful time but sometimes I think it vanished like a fairy tale.

I think about this big picture often. I have a personal relationship to it, after all. But if I'm honest it's the domestic dramas that preoccupy me the most. After the Paralympics, and my rallying cry on *SPOTY*, I suppose I could have developed a taste for politics. I didn't though because, apart from work, Nick and I were having a serious debate. Should we or should we not have a little brother and sister for Oscar? Coming from the family I did, I wanted him to have the fun from siblings that I'd had. Yet I was over forty and knew it would not be a foregone conclusion I'd get pregnant. We went through the pros and cons for ages, factoring in the joy and sense of completion versus the exhaustion of four million nappies. We couldn't make up our minds.

It's a dilemma that many women involved in careers they enjoy have to wrestle with, and I certainly identify with them. The freedom and fulfilment of work is fantastic, but how do you offset that against the love and fulfilment of parenthood, especially when you're from a big family yourself? In the end it was one of my friends from my old NCT class, Karen, who encapsulated my thinking: 'You're never going to regret having another child. But you might regret not having one.'

From the summer of 2014 onwards we were trying, but

nothing happened. I had an operation to remove a polyp around Christmastime and – good old festive cheer – discovered I was pregnant in the New Year. We didn't tell anyone except Mum at the beginning – it was too early – but everybody was round our house one Sunday at the end of January and it seemed too good an opportunity to keep it to ourselves. Cue happiness and huge surprise, given the pressure on our lives already.

I was just about to go away with the girls to Dubai when I had my first seven-week scan. Nick came with me. I felt fine. We were expecting everything to be OK but we weren't that fortunate.

'I can't seem to find a heartbeat,' were the words I vividly remember being told and I can still see the small reception area where Nick and I stood, not talking, while MTV played some blaring tune on a small screen and another expectant couple held hands, smiling.

I'd booked an appointment with a midwife for the next day, thinking I'd be talking about preliminary arrangements for the birth. I was so confused, but it seemed a good idea to go and speak to her. Was I or wasn't I pregnant?

'Oh congratulations!' she said as I walked through the door, which made me immediately burst into tears. She backed up the words we'd heard the day before, that a non-audible heartbeat was no definite proof we'd lost the baby. It might be too early to tell. 'Go on your holiday,' she said, 'and we'll do another scan when you get back.'

I went on my Dubai holiday but I wasn't really there. I was constantly somewhere in my own head, wondering and fearing the outcome. Just to be on the safe side, I drank non-alcoholic beer. Coming home for the second scan was nerve-racking. We had to have the answer but I was frightened of it at the same time. It confirmed what I already knew in my heart of hearts. We'd lost the baby and I'd need another procedure, something the medical profession calls an ERPC, to save telling you it stands for the Evacuation of Retained Products of Conception. I understand the need for scientific detachment, but to Nick and I, our baby was gone; those were our words.

The whole thing was very sad. The procedure was in the same hospital, Stoke Mandeville, where I'd had Oscar. The same curtains round the beds. Just the very sight of them reminded me of lying with a little baby beside me and walking out with a bundle in my arms. Mum was with me. We'd be going home on our own this time.

Despite trying for the next six months, nothing happened, and I began to research information on IVF treatment late at night when I should have been in bed. I knew time was running out and, given the number of operations I'd had in my life, it could well have been internal scar tissue that was causing the problem. A visit to Harley Street later (literally chandeliers in the room and wine with dinner) and another operation, and Nick and I embarked on our first session of IVF.

It's no good pretending it's not gruelling because it is. It required lots of internals, injecting myself with drugs in my stomach, and my hormones were all over the place. Nick was virtually paranoid with the thought he might have to take drugs too. He can't even take a multivitamin without feeling faint. I said: 'Don't worry, love, just keep taking the Stella.'

We tried but it failed and I reluctantly let that dream go. It's still there in the back of my mind that I'd love Oscar to have a brother and sister like I did, but it's not going to happen now. If we'd had a little girl we'd have called her Daisy. We've acquired a Daisy, but she's hairier than I'd originally planned, being a black Labrador puppy. It makes me smile when I hear Oscar calling her his 'baby sister'. It's the best we could do, and we'll just have to be creative and adopt a family for him among our friends and relatives. The important thing is we know how lucky we are to have Oscar, a beautiful, healthy and funny little boy. That's what counts.

I tend to look forward not back. I refuse to dwell on painful things. Yet when the tenth anniversary of 7/7 came round I had still not yet set foot on the tube. If I needed to go into London I drove, thanks to disabled parking spaces. I didn't have to confront the memories from a decade ago.

It couldn't go on forever, this boycott, but I knew I'd have to wait until I was ready. It was two tickets to Wimbledon that did it. All these years of being a Londoner and I'd never been to the world's most famous tennis championships, but two tickets to the men's semi-finals were mine and Nick's if we cared to have them. We did care.

This coincided, to the day, with the tenth commemoration of the bombings and I felt this new step was possible. Who better to help me get over a hurdle like this than two of my absolute sporting heroes, Roger Federer and Andy Murray.

Nick and I tried to make everything as low-key and relaxed as possible. We took the overland train into London, with coffee and newspapers to while away the journey. I was wearing my legs and my wheelchair was folded alongside me. As we rattled towards London the train gradually filled with people whose pearls and picnics hinted at their destination being the same as ours. Our plan was to change at Clapham Junction but, as we pulled into West Brompton, the picnics and pearls evacuated.

'Nick!' I nudged him. 'Look, d'you think these people are going to Wimbledon?'

He peered over this paper. 'Oh, yeah, maybe they are.'

'Shall we get off here then?' I said, knowing we'd need to move in a hurry. Then I looked out of the window and saw the famous tube sign. Just a blue line through a red ring, but it gave me a sudden tremor.

I refused to think about its significance. We darted off the train and the doors clanged behind us.

'Are you going to be all right?' Nick asked.

I thought about it. Was I going to be all right?

'Yes, I'm excited,' I decided.

Typically for London Transport the lift wasn't working so we had to lug my wheelchair up and down stairs until we finally stood on the tube platform. I said to Nick, who had his camera, as usual, 'We should really have a picture of this.' Our fellow travellers must have wondered why this apparently mad tourist insisted on having her photo taken as a perfectly ordinary District line train came into view behind her. I still have that picture and I love the fact that I'm smiling.

The carriages rushed in, the wind gushing around them. It felt and sounded so familiar and yet I hadn't experience this for a decade. The doors opened and I walked on. That felt good. I walked on legs made of wires and metal instead of flesh and blood, but what's the difference as long as you can walk at all.

I glanced, I couldn't help it, at the seat I'd sat in that fatal morning. For just a split second I recalled the scene of carnage and devastation. The darkness and the smoke and the cries and the confusion. Mercifully Brompton Road was an open-air tube station. It was a lovely sunny day and Nick was clicking away with his camera. It was all right. I was safe. It wasn't going to happen again.

When we roared into a tunnel for the first time I felt a flickering of nerves, but the overwhelming feeling was one of happiness. We reached Wimbledon and then we were like every other couple getting off a train, swarming towards the exit, excited to see the tennis, looking forward to our first glass of champagne . . .

'Well done, babe,' Nick said, and gave me a hug. 'I'm really proud of you.'

I was proud too, I suppose. And relieved. Wimbledon was fabulous. Roger has never looked more gorgeous. My phone exploded with Twitter messages of congratulations. Another milestone accomplished.

I love being one of the GB 'floor cleaners' and want to carry on playing because I love the sport and my teammates so much. I have the perfect answer to anyone who says, 'Are you kidding? At your age!' I've been told there's a woman on the Slovenian volleyball team who's the same age as my mum. I'll preserve my mother's dignity by not revealing the exact number but it's got a (lucky) seven in it.

But by mid 2017, I knew the time felt right to retire as captain. I've enjoyed every moment. I've earned nearly ninety caps and I am the most capped female in the history of British sitting volleyball. Above all it's been tremendous fun with a great group of girls. Vicky Widdup, my vice captain, will do a fantastic job of stepping up into the leadership role. I remember with fondness and gratitude all those times leading up to the London Games when I could splurge out my feelings to her. She was and will remain a really good mate. British Volleyball are recruiting hard for new players, and I will stick around as a player and a mentor for as long as they need me. I'm quite a long way off my seventies.

And it was just like old times when one of my last tournaments took me to Finland again with Claire. Both in our forties; both laughing at the fact that the team still seemed have the very same tactical conundrums we had back in London. No naked male Slovakians this time, though, which was a shame.

Being a sportswoman not long after a time when I'd worried about just being human again has been a highlight of my life. There is no doubt sport helped save me. It healed me. It was one of the huge ironies that I had to lose two legs, usually considered quite valuable in sport, to take part in the greatest sporting show on earth.

Yet I'm aware of the difference between myself and other ex-professional sportswomen. And I don't mean physically. Yes, athleticism was important; it was empowering to feel healthy, fit and packed with protein, courtesy of all those boiled eggs. But the greatest power sport gave me was confidence, motivation, self-belief. It made sense of something inherently insane – the murdering and maiming of strangers. It allowed me to achieve a dream I never remotely imagined possible. And, just as important, maybe more so, it allowed me the opportunity to give something amazingly special back to my family.

Few people love London more than my mum and dad. If I was ever going to make it up to them for the anguish they've suffered because of me, then something involving

London, royalty, sport, history and a fabulous excuse for a party was perfect.

And the healing extended further in my eyes, right across this great capital city where the effects of 7/7 could have made Londoners and visitors afraid or at least wary. They reckoned tourists stayed away for a while for fear of another attack. But one giant sporting event – which turned into a month-long celebration where people hugged strangers and jumped on and off trains without a second thought – changed all that.

The after-effects have gone on and on for me like ripples in a pond. A posh envelope arrived one morning in 2016 with a stamped message on the front: 'On Her Majesty's Service'. What had I done? I wondered. Not another speeding course, surely. I opened it carefully and had to reread it about a dozen times. It continued to say the same thing: 'The Prime Minister has put your name forward to the Queen for an MBE ...' I bet they were going to tell me I couldn't tell anyone. Sure enough ... I did my best. It was minutes before I told Nick and days before I told Mum and Dad, who both cried.

I planned the day meticulously. Four tickets bumped up to five so that Oscar could come; table for fourteen booked at a Gordon Ramsay restaurant for after the ceremony as a treat for my wonderful family; and a flight back the night before from Gran Canaria, so I'd have plenty of time to have my hair done and dress at a leisurely pace (with a suntan) in the morning.

They said it was the worst storm suffered by Gran Canaria in fifty years. How typical was that! Our flight home was horrendously delayed and then police brought all the traffic on our particular section of the M25 to a standstill. I know this was aimed at me because we were in the very front line of the jam. I had to resist the urge to wind down the window and shout, 'I've got an appointment with your monarch, mate, first thing tomorrow! Let me go.'

The following morning the anticipated serenity was replaced by chaotic action as four of us piled into the taxi – we were meeting Dad at the palace – and I had to do my make-up precariously en route. Oscar was wearing a new suit and brogues and kept telling me, over and over, 'I'm so excited about today. I love you so much and I'm so proud of you, Mummy.'

It brought to mind all those motorway sobbing fits on my way to volleyball training, convinced Oscar would be inescapably damaged by my absence. I needn't have worried after all. He is a smashing, sweet, happy boy. If he knows the dialogue of every *Star Wars* episode then that's Nick's doing, and probably all to the good.

Dad was outside Buckingham Palace waiting for us. He'd probably been there since midnight. As we walked across the gravel drive – I noted that the Queen still hasn't taken my advice on the size of her stones – my attention was taken by those little sentry boxes where the guards normally stand. They were empty on this occasion.

'Quick, Oscar, get in one of those for a photo,' I whispered, sending him on the mission.

A policeman was on us like a flash. 'Excuse me, no photos,' he said politely.

'Oh, sorry,' I said. 'Quick, Oscar, get out of there.'

Inside the Palace we were advised that it would be the Princess Royal performing the ceremony and not the Queen. I explained to Oscar and he didn't seem put out. 'Don't worry,' he said, 'I've just seen the Queen. She was around that corner and she waved at me.'

I don't think she did but I admired his imagination.

The family went one way and I went the other, to be instructed about curtseying and walking backwards. I put a hand up and said I couldn't do either of those things with any degree of safety on my legs. Maybe they remembered me from Prince Charles's terrace because they said it was quite all right – all I had to do was nod.

So I had my moment collecting a very precious medal, even if it wasn't a Paralympic one. Of course it would have been great to have a gold medal round my neck but I don't need it. I have my own version, and it's on display in my hall: a framed photo of my family that day in the Excel Arena. Oscar on Nick's shoulders, holding up his painted sign. Mum with her tissue on standby. Dad with his ruddy great Slimming World banner.

Two weeks later Nick drove me to north London, clearly sworn to secrecy, and promising 'a surprise'. Being a cabbie's daughter, I tried to work out where we were going and why. I guessed a restaurant with the family. Not even close. It was a pub, for a start, filled with loads of my mates, some going way back in time to clubbing days: Joe, the 'man I went home with' on the night I met my husband; various parents of friends, including the Wrath-of-Rita, just hordes of people all gathered together by those partners in crime, Alex, Sarah and Michelle. Some I hadn't seen for years; half a lifetime. It was overwhelming.

There was a massive cake with a picture of me on top complete with prosthetic legs and giant gold helium balloons not much smaller than me with the letters M, B and E emblazoned on them. The face of the Uber driver who had to take me back to my parked car the next morning from Balham, where I'd been staying with one of the girls, was a picture.

'So that bag's got a giant cake in it, this ones got two legs in it, then it's just those three zeppelin-sized balloons . . . and me.'

I don't really know what's next. I don't have a plan. I'd like to carry on being a GB player and take up a new mentor role within the team, as well as remain involved in the sporting world. Sport gave me so much, and I have a duty to share that. Hopefully the powers-that-be will realise its value. It gave me back my confidence and self-belief. I'm always going to bang on about its power.

I hope my former Paralympic teammates, the ones I

still know and the ones I've lost touch with, are happy and fulfilled in whatever they are doing now. It gives me huge pleasure that Emma finally achieved her gold medal. She just needed to get off the court with us and get on the water on her own. Claire Harvey took up field sports and finished fourth in the shot put at the 2015 IPC World Championships and would have made Rio but for an injury. Jodi opened a guest house in Uganda. Julie competed as a sprinter in Rio for British Athletics, and I'm sure I saw Jay on a TV programme a while back about people who regretted their tattoos.

My philosophy these days is simple: be happy. Be positive. Have belief. If you believe in something it can happen. Tracey reminded me of a card I gave her a week after coming out of my coma. It was her birthday and Mum had secretly bought me the card to write in, if I could. 'Love you, Sis', I'd written, which was quite a feat in itself. 'Don't worry. We'll be running round the park together next year.' I'm amazed at the strength of my optimism. You could argue it was the drugs but I have tried to live up to it ever since.

It all comes back to the coincidences. Once you truly believe you are on the right path, nothing in the world will deflect you. I even wonder about the nail bomb at the Admiral Duncan pub in Soho, in 1999, when three people were killed and dozens more injured. I was in Quo Vadis round the corner and we were evacuated from the bar. I remember doing what everyone did on 7/7. I was trying to get through to my mum and dad to let them know I was OK but the networks were down. We were walking down the street passing people with blood all over their faces. I can't say it was a premonition from a different point of view; that would sound ridiculous. But it's still a coincidence.

I list them sometimes. I can't help it. Being immersed in reading about the Olympics at the very moment the bomb detonated. Travelling to my first volleyball international on 7 July. Oscar being due on 7 July. My volleyball club backing onto The Royal London. My old hospital room in Roehampton being visible from the GB training base. The bus that took us to the Olympic Village flashing past Aldgate Station, Bart's and The Royal London Hospital in quick succession. The view of my old office in Tower Hill from City Hall when the GB squad was announced. Competing in the Paralympics seven years after 7/7. Wearing the No.7 shirt . . . someone else might see them as irrelevant. Not me.

I've discovered all kinds of tiny circumstances over the years – through conversations with people or by following the inquest – which, if they had changed one iota, I wouldn't be here. I jumped onto that train carriage but the seat I chose, my favourite seat, was behind a pane of glass in the corner. Without that shield the police are sure Andy and I would have been killed. The bomber, for some reason, had taken off his rucksack containing the explosives and put it on the floor. That's why there were so many leg injuries. Had he worn it on his chest, Andy and I would be dead.

No wonder I've come to believe it was fate, but I don't torment myself with the idea that I should have changed what I did that morning. I could drive myself mad with 'if only's. If I'd got up in the morning when my alarm went off instead of having ten more minutes in bed. If I'd power-walked slightly slower or faster to Harringay Station. If I'd decided to take the bus from Old Street because the Northern line was partly down that day. If I'd decided against taking the Circle line from Moorgate. If I hadn't run up that escalator. If I hadn't jumped on the second carriage, because I normally sat at the back of the train, as it was nearer to the stairway at Tower Hill. If the train had been packed and I'd had to stand. If Liz hadn't been the amazing, courageous woman she is. If that man hadn't found that belt. If my blood hadn't drained weirdly slowly . . . all those ifs. I binned them. There was nothing I could have done to stop what happened that day. It was fate. Even if it really wasn't, that thought has been hugely beneficial to me.

I have no idea what the future holds. I'll carry on working for as long as it lasts. I realise my story, being part of something so resonant and memorable, has given me a voice and opportunity I shouldn't ignore. Every adult UK citizen surely remembers where they were on that day in July 2005. Whether they were caught up in the bombings themselves, or trying to ring someone, or trying to get a cab to go home because the entire London transport network had ground to a halt, or even just watching the horror unfold on TV, people remember where they were, what they did, who they rang. Whenever I give a talk someone will come up to me afterwards and tell me their story, just as I've told them mine. It's an instant connection. I love the rapport. It's important to me to go on doing this – to relate to people. Touch people.

These connections reveal the small world we inhabit. 7/7 is such a huge cultural landmark in our lives that all sorts of random people I meet turn out to have a connection with it. It could be two old dears talking in a doctor's surgery about their mate's daughter who was caught up in it, and then it turns out they go to the same dance hall as my dad. Or I'm talking to my speaker agent, a fabulous woman called Helen, and she's just talked to a client whose living room is being painted by one of the firemen that rescued me.

It's one of the things that Nick and I have in common, an innate belief in the connectedness of things. From worrying about the differences between Nick and I at the beginning of our relationship, I now realise they bring us strength as well as laughter. There are times when we get frustrated with one another. I can't believe he spends so long analysing everything and he can't believe I never do. He doesn't like life taking him by surprise whereas I love it.

Another classic difference is our attitude to our home town. Objectively, Tring is a small market town in Hertfordshire, nestling in a gap between the Chiltern Hills. I think it's a village and he always says, 'No, it's a town.'

'What are you talking about?' I ask him. 'Anywhere that's only got ten shops must be a village!'

Like all couples we need more time together. But we're happy. We love each other. One of our ambitions is to one day build our own home deeper into the countryside. 'Not too deep,' I tell him.

His sticking point is he must have a fireplace with a dog in front of it and a lovely view outside the window. We now have a dog, so I'm promising to work on the rest of it. I look at him sometimes and think, God, how did you get through the terrible experience you suffered because of what happened to me? He always says I've got 'more front than Sainsbury's', but he saw something more vulnerable on the inside. He's the opposite. He's a gentle soul with the inner strength of a survivor.

It makes me laugh when I hear him call up to Oscar, exasperated, in the morning when we're trying to get him off to school: 'Come on, Oscar! You're away with the fairies.'

I think to myself, Well, you can't really blame the boy when his father's away with the fairies himself half the time on some creative mission and I have a habit of leaving everything to the last possible minute. Perhaps Oscar will be spared his parents' excesses. All we want is for him to be happy and fulfilled in the long run – and if I do get to be a droid in *Star Wars* for him so much the better.

I'm sometimes asked a simple question: don't you wish you could go back to that morning on 7/7 and change the outcome? The answer is simple. No, I don't. I didn't feel like that in the first couple of years. I would have done anything to rewind time (like in *Doctor Who*, Oscar would say) and be transformed back to a woman with legs again.

But now I wouldn't change it. I've seen the best and worst of human nature. Not just seen it, nearly died and lived because of it. I have achieved things beyond my craziest imagining, met a stream of amazing and memorable people, have loads of friends who mean the world to me, adore my wonderful family, and my job description is 'talking' – how perfect is that?

Stuff happens. It's not the stuff that's important; it's how you deal with it. I dealt with it as well as I could: headfirst and hopeful. I don't look back except in gratitude to all the people who have helped, loved and supported me. I'm proof, literally living proof, that anything is possible.

Acknowledgements

Sitting down to write this book I had no idea what emotions and memories would come swirling back for me and my family. It's been an extraordinary experience to remember all those who have been part of my life and recovery and it's hard to know how to begin to express all the gratitude I feel.

So let me first thank the people on that day of the bombings in 2005 who were prepared to risk their lives to save others. They had no idea if secondary devices had been deployed but they came down into the underground to find us anyway. My sincere gratitude to all the emergency services who were involved in the rescue and the fantastic NHS staff who put us back together again.

Heartfelt thanks to all those members of the public who helped the injured on that day and especially to the lovely Liz Kenworthy, the off-duty policewoman whose bravery and humanity led her to come to my rescue. You held my hand and stayed with me, risking your own life. Your quick thinking in such a scene of carnage undoubtedly saved my life. You're forever in my heart as my guardian angel.

To Hasu Patel, a doctor at The Royal London Hospital, whose skill as a surgeon saved my life. Thank you, Hasu, for your dedication, being there for my family and for providing the friendly face I woke up to every morning that filled me with hope.

I can't thank The Royal London enough for the care I received. Big thanks to all the staff who amused me by popping their heads round the door to say, 'Oh, you don't remember me Martine, do you? But I operated on you . . .' How many operations did I have! Special thanks to James, my intensive care nurse who was the first person to tell me I'd lost my legs, which he did with such gentle compassion, and to all the other nurses, doctors, physios and OTs, who looked after me so brilliantly. Apologies to the ICU nurse I accused of stealing my blood. I'm sure you know that was just the morphine talking.

Thanks also for the support of my fellow patients and 7/7 survivors that I met in Harrison Ward at The Royal London and Queen Mary Hospital in Roehampton: Andy Brown, Danny Biddle, Philip Patsalos, Thelma Stober, Kira Mason – and also to my 'twin', Jeannette Adu-Bobie, who became such a good friend, while sharing laughs and the frustrations of learning to cope with our injuries.

ACKNOWLEDGEMENTS

To all the staff at the Queen Mary where I learned to walk again – you have my respect, love and gratitude for getting me back up on my new feet. Thank you especially, my fantastic physio Maggie, for teaching me to walk again and, more than that, being a shoulder to cry on and a lifelong friend. How perfect is the fact that your new married name is 'Mrs. Walker'?!

Everyone at Roehampton helped my family and me navigate this new world as alien at first as stepping on Mars. I'm forever indebted to the patients, doctors, physios, OTs, technicians, my fantastic social worker, Carol, and John Sullivan, my prosthetic manager and all his protégées. I'm especially grateful to John for making me two inches taller on my wedding day as the man I was marrying is six foot three. Also, Mary Jane, Sarah, Mary, Fiona, Moira and all who worked in the 'walking school'. Many thanks to Dr Soori, not only for his world-renowned expertise in leg amputees, but for the bacon sandwiches he bought us all as a treat twice a week. Finally, to Debbie on the admin desk, a special thanks for all those times I wandered down to have gossip about absolutely nothing.

To Jim, our family liaison police officer, thank you for being such a friend to the family and helping us all through one of the toughest times of our lives with your down-to-earth kindness and practicality.

To Keith Barrett at Irwin Mitchell, very many thanks for your *pro bono* work and calm expertise at a scary time.

So many people in so many ways helped me along in those dark, confusing days and you were certainly one of them.

To everyone at my old company, CNet, and my fantastic boss, Kathy Teo, thank you for supporting me for two years and helping me try to come back to work after my recovery. I know what happened to me that day must have been a terrible shock to all of you too, but you were never less than completely understanding and I will always appreciate that.

Thanks to those who supported both me and my whole family through such a terrible time. People were amazingly kind in so many different ways – old school friends, former work colleagues, my old bosses, friends of friends and people whose lives had converged with mine for just a little while. My mum and dad too were really lifted by the generosity of their own friends. My mum's best mate Maria would take her out for the day and Lianne's dad, Keith, went to the trouble of organising a fundraiser for us. Those gestures were hugely appreciated and made a real difference to us all.

So did the wonderful support of Nick's old school friends – Richard, Darren, Tim and Mark, who have always been there, but especially for Nick in those very early days. And of course Jacqui for helping Sarah search for me when I was missing.

And thank you to the general public; the well-wishers who took the time and trouble to send me cards, flowers, books, letters – all tokens of wonderful kindness from people who didn't even know me. The walls in my room at the Douglas Bader unit were covered so that you couldn't see an inch of the 1970s wallpaper. Every letter gave me new strength. After something so horrific, it completely restored my faith in human decency and generosity.

To journalists Sandra Laville of the *Guardian* and Lucy Panton and Sara Nuwar of the (then) *News of the World*, who covered my story from the very early days when I was barely over the worst of my injuries; I have to thank you for treating me with such empathy and sensitivity. Journalists don't always get the greatest of accolades but you were there for all the big milestones in my life: hospital, marriage, Oscar. It could have been intrusive and awkward but thanks to you it never was. I'm grateful you helped me share my story in the way I wanted to, always emphasising that good could come from bad.

Thank you to Kirstie Allsopp, Phil Spencer and everyone on the team at *Location, Location* for finding us our new family home. It was great fun and, Phil, I still have a piece of woodwormed timber as a souvenir for you!

Thank you to the Flying Scholarships for the Disabled charity, Disability Snowsport UK, the Douglas Bader Foundation, Queen Mary's Hospital and Sport Relief for providing me with opportunities of a lifetime.

To Martin Corck and the wonderful Helen Williams for

helping me build my career with your organisational brilliance and the odd kick up the backside when required. I really don't know what I would do without you.

To all the charities I work with as an ambassador, many thanks for giving me the chance to pay back all the amazing benefits I've received. To St Bartholomew's and Royal London hospitals – one that brought me into this world and the other that stopped me leaving it – The Diana Awards, Pepper Foundation, Team London, the Universities of York and East London for my honorary doctorates, Breakthrough Breast Cancer Inspiration Awards, the *Guardian* and *Observer* Ethical Awards.

To the GB women's sitting volleyball team – thanks for sharing an amazing adventure all the way to London 2012 and beyond, and for the most non-PC laughs that helped us all accept who we are. I'm privileged to have discovered the healing power of sport beside you. Special appreciation too goes to Ian Legrand, Karen Hung and the entire support team for their commitment, dedication and belief in us. Thanks, too, to the British Paralympic Association, Volleyball England and all those who supported us on our way – the team managers, physios, strength and conditioning coaches and psychologists, right through to the volunteer 'ball shaggers', as the ball collectors are called. It has to be the ultimate in dedicated volunteering, to give up your spare time for para sport, only to be given the title 'ball shagger'. They are appreciated, one and all.

ACKNOWLEDGEMENTS

A massive thank you must go to the Great British public whose phenomenal enthusiasm made the London Paralympics such an unforgettable success. They and the volunteers created an atmosphere that brought joy to the nation for a whole fortnight. It was a magical time.

Thank you to the BBC for giving me my first opportunity to commentate at the inaugural Invictus Games in the Olympic Park in 2014. It was brilliant to be back somewhere so special and work with the lovely Jonathan Legard, who looked after me. I was more than thrilled to cover the next Games in Florida too with the equally lovely Chris Mitchell.

I must thank Channel 4 and Sunset+Vine, especially Michael Cole, for another opportunity of a lifetime when they selected me as a roving reporter on their team for the Rio Paralympics. It was an awesome experience beginning with my media training with Bright Spark Media. I'm glad I provided you with a popular 'How Not To Do It' clip for all your future trainees.

Thanks for the support to all the team in Brazil, especially my fellow 'rovers', Sean Rose, Sophia Warner and Jordan Jarrett-Bryan, not forgetting cameraman Keith and sound man Andrew who helped remove the stress and nerves with their relaxed professionalism. I'm glad I shared my one afternoon off at the beach with you.

I am so lucky to have the friends I have – wonderful people who understood at the beginning, when things were very raw, that I just couldn't face seeing them. I couldn't even look at myself let alone have my best friends see me that way. I know it must have been painful for them all. So thank you for giving me the space to recover and then resume the old fun when I was ready.

I hope my friends know how much I love and appreciate them. Even though my career is now built around talking, I'm still pretty rubbish on the phone, but whenever we see each other we just pick up from where we left off. This has to include my 'besties' from schooldays – Lianne Morrison, my godmother Michelle Sofocli, the Meads (Claire, Kelly and Jo) – Shirley Pinnock, Tara Holland, Alison Taylor, Juliette Murray – who have been part of my life for the last thirty-to-forty years. I'm so lucky to have them. The bond we share will always be there. For all the wonderful memories, the umpteen houses we shared and the clubs we frequented in the 1990s – looking forward to the next forty years!

I also have to include Alex Farrell, thank you for being the best boss in the world and a friend for life. So sorry I missed your wedding but I hope we've made up for it since in a million ways. Thank you for always being there, being the witty, kind, empathetic Welsh girl you are, and for attempting to pick me up numerous times after falling out of my chair! And to Sarah Jones for being the determined, loving and wonderful character you are. Thank you for tirelessly searching for me in the terrible aftermath of the bombings. Thank you for all the help with PR in the early days and blagging Nick and I a fabulous honeymoon courtesy of Richard Branson – thank you Richard, too. And thank you Jenny Porterfield, fellow Londoner, with your down-to-earth attitude, strength and loyalty, who, after a chance meeting sixteen years ago, has now become a life-long friend.

To the lovely friends who organised and came to my surprise MBE party – amazing friends, amazing party, amazing cake and the biggest MBE balloons I have ever seen (thank you Sarah Mason). I don't know how you made Nick swear not to tell me about it but it worked – I had no idea at all!

Thank you to all our friends in Tring, our hometown, including my NCT mates, Alex, Karen, Maija, Kike and Celia. With twelve children between us now, playdates are slightly more hectic compared to the early days. The same thanks to the school mums and, of course, to my mate Jennie and our adopted Mosley family – thank you for the shared school runs, Stella nights and Spanish holidays.

To the friends I haven't seen for a while, including Harri and Jillian, 'Duck'n'Rice' Claire, Joe, Anthony and Scot, the Crouch End lot and so many others, you know who you are. Life is just whizzing by but we will meet up for that beer one day.

I feel blessed to have so many good friends. You know who you are and I love each and every one of you.

It's been terrific working with everyone at publishers Simon & Schuster to produce this book, especially Kerri Sharp, Nicki Crossley, Harriet Dobson and Liz Marvin. Many thanks also to Rory Scarfe from Furniss Lawton for being so supportive from the start, and I'm specially grateful to Sheree and photographer Sophia Spring for dropping everything they were doing at short notice to convert my living room into a photo studio and create such a brilliant book cover.

To Sue Mott, thank you for your patience, perseverance and support in writing this book over what feels like the last ten years! Thank you for being the lovely lady you are and for speaking to my family so often you've now become an honorary Wrighty.

Ultimately, I am who I am because of my family. They've loved me and supported me throughout everything. I've learned my strength, love, humour and kindness through them. I don't know what I would do without them.

So to my dear mum, thank you for being the best mum and nanny in the world and for being my inspiration. You've shown me nothing but love, strength, courage and devotion all my life and especially when I needed it most. And, on top of all that, you're still our wonderful 'washing fairy'.

To my dear dad, thank you for your love, strength and support and our shared sense of humour. Thank you for all those childhood memories and swinging me round the dance floor to Frank Sinatra at any opportunity. And of course for going out for those sausage rolls in hospital when I couldn't face the thought of eating anything else.

To my sister, Tracey, I love you for your huge strength, support and, of course, your organisation. Sorry I missed your fiftieth birthday while I was at the Paralympics in London but a least you had a broom with my cardboard face on it! We've grown closer and closer through the years and I'll never forget all those road trips round the M25 on a Friday afternoon when I was allowed out of hospital at weekends. Thank you for always helping out with Oscar, especially during the Paralympics when you helped keep my husband sane.

To my big bro Grant – thank you for being the elder brother who didn't mind getting stuck with me when we were growing up. It was wonderful to have a big brother with the same mental age as me! I will always remember your belief in me during those dark days and it helped me so much to find the strength to recover. Thanks too for the bracelet you bought me to remind me that I could achieve my dreams after all.

To the rest of my family – thank you Maureen, for always being there and for your magical patience in dealing with my lovely dad! And Alley for your support and for being there for Grant at the hardest of times.

To my fabulous nephews and nieces: Alicia, Tyler, Matilda, Felix and, more recently, Alicia's fiancé Lewis, a million thanks for your continued kisses and cuddles. It can't have been easy to see me in hospital. I remember you, Alicia, telling me that it wasn't the shock of seeing me with no legs but the sight of me with blood-filled eyes that scared you. Still, those days are over. I love you all and remember, stick with your auntie and you'll never have to queue up at a theme park again!

And, of course, love and thanks to the Wiltshires – Pete, Celia, Joanne and Simon – for welcoming me with open arms into their family and always being there for us.

To my husband Nick, I love you with all my heart and you know how much you mean to me. Thank you for always picking me up – sometimes literally! You have my eternal appreciation for your patience, love and support, for being there when things got tough and for having the courage not to look for a way out but a way forward. We may be different but we have an incredible strength few other couples have. I love you for supporting me in my dreams, for being a great husband, father and friend.

To my son Oscar, thank you for making my heart melt every day and for the best cuddles in the world. Life doesn't get much better than when your seven-year-old says, 'I love you so much and I'm so proud of you, Mummy'. You are my everything and I love you to the moon and stars × infinity.

Through all the different things I've done in the last twelve years I've been privileged to meet the most amazing people, some famous, some not, who have shared their stories with me. Thank you for the insights you have given me and for the opportunity to get to know you – even in passing. It gives me great hope and strength to know there are so many lovely people out there.

Last but not least, to the fifty-two people that lost their lives on that fateful day: you and your families will always be in my thoughts. And in my heart.

Picture credits

First section

Page 1: Top row © John Frost Newspapers; bottom row © Getty Images

Page 2: © Author's own collection

Page 3: © Author's own collection

Page 4: © Author's own collection

Page 5: Top left © Author's own collection; top right and middle row © ITV/REX/SHUTTERSTOCK; bottom row © Author's own collection

Page 6: © Author's own collection

Page 7: © Author's own collection

Page 8: © Author's own collection

Second section

Page 9: Top row © Getty Images; middle row © Author's own collection; bottom row © DAILY MAIL/REX/SHUTTERSTOCK

Page 10: Top and middle row © Author's own; bottom row © Getty Images

Page 11: © Author's own collection

Page 12: Top left © Sam Friedrich/Acumen Images, rest of page © Author's own collection

Page 13: © Author's own collection

Page 14: © Author's own collection

Page 15: © Author's own collection

Page 16: © Author's own collection